Lori Matzke

HOME STAGING

CREATING BUYER-FRIENDLY ROOMS

TO SELL YOUR HOUSE.

HOME STAGING

ACKNOWLEDGEMENTS

As with any major undertaking, and most certainly as this book was for me, there are many 'winds beneath the wings' of the final product. I would like to take this time to express my sincere and heartfelt thanks to all those who had a hand in helping to shape this publication.

A SPECIAL THANKS...

To all the Homeowners, for allowing me to invade their privacy, and are now giving strangers a glimpse of their home through this book. It's not easy inviting an outsider in. Even tougher when there's a photographer in tow. A million thanks for your kindness, flexibility, help, and hospitality. Major kudos to **Tom, Nancy, Bill, Mrs. Bill, Linda, Fran, Emily, Maria, Chris, Judy, Russ, Tim, Anna, Ross, Katie,** and the **Roitenberg Residence.** You all deserve a standing ovation!

To the Center Stage Home Affiliates, for lifting me onward and upward while understanding my time commitment to this project without complaint. You are truly "The Dream Team" and the most talented, professional group of individuals in the industry. I couldn't have asked for more.

To Eric Schmid of Bufflehead Web Design, for taking on the challenge of deciphering my cryptic notes and managing to come up with the perfect solution every time. You are by far the most generous, easy-going person I have ever met. How on earth do you put up with me?

To Rollin Alm, James Gross, and Karl Herber, for allowing me access to your many beautiful works of art. **And to Rebecca Alm,** for always accommodating my terrible sense of timing with a smile.

To Hans Hirshfield and Jeff Lien of Hirshfield's Paint and Wallcovering, Inc., for making such a swift management decision and putting it into play. "If it were easy, anyone could do it!"

To **Sandi Roth** of *MY TURN II - Used, Unique, Antique Furniture, Etc.* Sandi, you are a one-woman show! How lucky for my life path to have crossed with yours.

To **Arlan Garvis,** whose stories, good humor, friendship, and genuine enthusiasm in my future I appreciated much more than I ever expressed. I told you I wouldn't forget.

To **Ryan Wood,** for lining up the 80's Contemporary, keeping my eye on upcoming endeavors, and lending an ear whenever I needed to talk, plot, or vent.

To **James and Laurie Gross,** for understanding and delivering exactly what I was looking for without having to explain myself a million times. Your creative minds and unwavering patience are just the right combination.

To **my sister and brother-in-law, "The Schlueter's,"** for dropping everything at a moment's notice whenever I needed a helping hand. Or a truck. Or both. But, that's what you get for buying an SUV!

And to my parents, Daniel and Hylma, for raising me in a home that always looked like an "after." My dad, who passed away far too young in 1994, had the uncanny ability to turn even the most distressed property into the envy of the neighborhood, and my mom was the perfect accomplice. With an eye for design and more energy than a rabbit, she has been blessed with a knack for keeping things fresh, new, and desperately clean. When I was a kid, a fun Saturday afternoon for me and my sister was helping Mom rearrange the living room. As a result, my poor dad fell over more ottomans in his lifetime than Dick Van Dyke! After coming home many late nights after a long day on the job, he eventually learned to turn the lights on before entering. It definitely took him a few trips to realize that the path he may have taken out the door after breakfast may no longer be the same path he should be taking back in after supper. While we may not have been the wealthiest family in town, somehow, through my parent's vision, innovative ideas, and hard work, you would never have known. We always had the nicest house on the block and beyond. Inside and out. Together they made a great team and instilled in me their deep passion for a well presented home. In memory of my wonderful dad, and to my mom's creative genes and steadfast support, this book is gratefully dedicated.

In 1999 after 8 years of work in accounting, a misguided path I still blame on my high school career counselor, I discovered home staging. Like pretty much everything else in my life, it was something I stumbled on quite by accident. Leaving a steady paycheck behind and after nearly a year of trying to find my way as a professional home organizer, it wasn't long before my ranking turned into nothing more than a glorified house keeper. An honest living, to be certain. But golly, what a drag. I am not sure if it was boredom, fumes from all the cleaning fluids, or a combination of both, but I am absolutely positive, as I bent over those grubby toilet bowls to scrub, I could literally feel my brain cells dying. A few months into my new stint as lady-with-a-mop, I was hired for one of those far and few between organizing jobs I had so coveted, a business venture I was still valiantly pursuing. But that one glorious day became the turning point I never quite expected.

Typically when hired to organize, I was brought in to do closets, cupboards, laundry rooms, and so on. Though a neat-nick at heart, what I usually ended up doing was rearranging the entire room. I mean, how could you have such a beautifully systemized closet when the rest of the place was still looking so darn tragic? On this particular day I was organizing a den for a family planning to sell their home. As I was busy shuffling through papers and books, and boxing up a collection of what could best be described as junk, I was introduced to their real estate agent. He took one look at my efforts and said, "Nice job. Great staging! Shows well." Huh? Did he say 'staging?' I had to think about that for a minute. Maybe I heard him wrong. Maybe I had already killed off so many brain cells that now my hearing was going too. Just to clarify, I asked him to please repeat. He said, "You know. Staging. Showing your house off to sell. It's all about first impressions." Then he smiled adding, "And you're pretty good at it." I didn't even know that's what I was doing, and will ya lookie there? I was already good at it. The wheels immediately started to turn. I was so excited I could have kissed him! To this day all I have to say is, "God bless you, Barry Berg!" Twenty-four hours later, I was marketing my new found skills to every real estate agent I could find. But just like organizing services, I found that selling professional home staging was a major uphill battle. Still a lot of hesitation among realtors in 1999. So for longer than I care to remember, I was Hazel by day and home staging expert, evenings and weekends. Just like Mata-Hari! Well. Sorta. I kept up that dual role until I just couldn't do it anymore. My home staging business had finally taken over to the point that I could hang up my rubber gloves for good. Admittedly, another glorious day in my life. And likely, not one I will ever forget.

Since that time, I've learned alot about home staging. I can definitely tell you, it is not interior design. And it is not redecorating. Home staging is essentially showing off your home by putting it's best features forward and appealing to as many potential buyers as possible. That's what it is. Deliberately playing up the house itself and thoughtfully creating a buyer-friendly environment. It's all about the potential buyer's perception of your house as they walk through, 10 to 15 minutes tops. It's all about first impressions. The fact is, you live in your home a lot differently than you would show it to sell. And I have yet to see a house that couldn't use at least a minor adjustment or two when that time comes. You have to realize that once your house is on the market, it is no longer your home. It's a product. To think you are going to garner a top offer by simply getting traffic through the door is naive. I've seen many, many realtors drop some major time, effort, and advertising bucks to promote a product that fell incredibly short of the hype, resulting in a lot of wasted energy and a disappointing outcome for all involved. Getting the showings is the easy part. Getting an offer is something altogether different. You have to put yourself in a certain frame of mind to prepare. You need to understand what potential buyers are there to see. Observe your house from their point of view to realistically understand what it is they are actually seeing. Then make the transformation accordingly. Every time your home is shown is an opportunity to sell. And every opportunity is a one-time shot. Once a prospective buyer has seen your house, they've seen it. And if they aren't initially excited by what they see, the opportunity has passed you by.

The houses featured in these chapters are real homes that yours truly staged for market. I have tried to include an assortment of styles and furnishings to give you a variety of viewpoints. With the exception of those that needed fresh paint or carpeting, and turning frugal into an art form, most were enhanced for under $100 in new accessories or finishing touches. What the owners already had on hand was re-invented. What they didn't have was often borrowed. And what couldn't be borrowed or purchased inexpensively was easily created. Aside from painting, they all took less than a day and most only a few short hours to complete. Keep in mind, these homes were not enhanced for the camera's eye or to show you the latest trends in design. They are a realistic view of what you can accomplish in your own home before putting it on the market.

What I've learned about home staging I am passing along to you. Through my experience, I have figured out how to show off the best aspects of a home and downplay the things that might not be too appealing. I've learned to streamline my efforts to make the process easy on the home owner. I've learned how to present a home like a prospective buyer would like to see it. And I've discovered many little tricks along the way. With that said, I am hoping you will find enough inspiration within to rethink the way you show your home before you put that "For Sale" sign on the lawn. And even more so, I hope you walk away with enough know-how to feel confident in getting there.

I am a firm believer that every home has potential. And I am a firm believer that any home can easily show it's true beauty with a little effort. All it takes is a game plan, some creativity, a jar of elbow grease, and the strong desire to show off your house in order to sell it quickly for the highest profit!

HOW DOES IT SELL MY HOUSE?

A few years ago, while looking to abandon apartment life for something I could call my own, I did what many others do in the initial steps of home-buying. I pre-qualified my loan so I knew exactly what I could afford. I narrowed down my search to several neighborhoods and then began scouring the Real Estate section in the Sunday paper to find out what was available. What I had in mind was a two-bedroom condo in close proximity to the heart of the city, a short commute to both work and fun. I was open to pretty much anything else. My needs were simple, and I was receptive to the possibilities. But even with so few requirements, it was still a tougher quest than I had originally counted on. Pretty slim pickin's, at the time. But out of the handful of listings I did find, several seemed quite encouraging. I eagerly made appointments to view the top three properties which I felt were the best prospects. Visions of "pride of ownership" danced in my head.

The first place I viewed was only a few blocks from my apartment building, located in a great neighborhood that I already loved. Priced on the higher end of my budget, though suspiciously under-priced for its location and size, it seemed like an absolute steal in theory. It was situated on a lake with nice bike and walking paths just a stones throw from the front door. And what the building itself lacked in exterior appeal, the listing within boasted to be "spacious and well maintained, with soaring ceilings and a view of the lake!!" With a perfect location and nearly 100 square feet more than either of the other properties I had planned to tour, what more could I ask for?

The realtor showed me in. And the best way I can describe my initial reaction is, "Yuck!" With limited furnishings and absolutely no clutter, save for the pile of shoes sitting next to the front door, it did

seem rather large. I'll give it that. But the moment I walked in, I was ready to turn around and walk right out. The main living area felt dingy, gloomy, and a little morose. The walls were still painted a pasty apartment white, and you didn't have to strain your eyes to see hints of drywall peering through. The carpeting was a matted gold loop that I have

no doubt had not been vacuumed, let alone cleaned, since it was first installed. I had a momentary flash of spending the first year in my new home without ever removing my slippers. The thought of my clean bare feet touching that grungy carpeting was just too unsettling to even think about.

Upon further inspection, and at the agent's coaxing, I took a quick glance up at the soaring ceilings I had so fervently anticipated. But what I noticed instead was a three foot crack coming down from the roof that seemed to have sprung an ugly leak. The crack was framed by what appeared to be a mildew stain that I am fairly certain had been cultivating itself for quite some time. Several new tributaries developing out of the main source immediately alerted me, the eruption was still alive and active. Visions of "pride of ownership" were quickly replaced by visions of the mounting repair bills I would be incurring.

While repainting would not be too difficult or pricey of an undertaking, I mentally contemplated how long a strip of duct tape might hold off a leak like that. My eye followed the stain down the wall and back to that ratty looking carpeting. Though the agent assured me the leak was "a minor repair" and "easy to fix." I wondered out loud, if that were true, "then why hasn't the owner repaired it?" So much for well-maintained. Exactly how essential were lakeside views and 100 extra square feet to my future happiness, anyway? I didn't need to see more.

My second appointment seemed more promising. Again, the location was just blocks from my apartment, only this time in the opposite direction. No lakeside view, but it was positioned smack-dab in the center of fabulous shopping, restaurants, and culture. Though the square footage of this two-bedroom was considerably less than the first, it was a pre-war brownstone with its original working fireplace, hardwood floors, and claw-foot tub in tact. What a find! From the outside, this building absolutely oozed of history and charm, and easily won my heart. It wasn't until I opened the front door that I questioned my devotion.

The realtor and I were immediately greeted by a big fluffy cat who made it very clear we would have to execute an Olympic-worthy gymnastics move over him if we planned to enter further. Once I aced my landing, I felt as if I had been transported directly to my grandmother's attic. I have never seen so much aged, cast-off furniture, so many knick-knacks and doilies, and just so darn much junk jammed into one small room in my life! It felt small. In fact, it felt downright cramped!

There were two large sofas in less than presentable condition facing each other on opposite walls. They were surrounded by a mismatched assortment of side tables and chairs, all of which looked as if they had succumbed to cat's need to sharpen his claws at one time or another. Every inch of wall space was absolutely plastered with pictures, photos, and memorabilia. It felt dizzying, not to mention claustrophobic. I found myself so busy checking out all the collections, I completely forgot why I came! The realtor had long moved on to the kitchen. I think I heard her mutter something about "subway tile," but her voice kind of trailed off in the background as I scrutinized a fairly sizable grouping of dusty snow-globes displayed on the mantle. Mantle?! The fireplace! There it was! I guess I just missed it, hidden there amidst all that other stuff.

I obligingly toured the rest of the rooms, partly out of respect for the realtor's time, but more so, I was curious to see what else we would find. Before I took another step I already knew, this place wasn't for me. It felt old. It felt crowded. There was hardly enough room to turn myself around, let alone invite in any visitors. The fireplace? I hadn't noticed. Hardwood floors? I don't recall. And I'm pretty sure there was a funky smell coming from the front hall closet. I was definitely not interested. "See ya, cat!"

My third appointment was for a condo located right downtown, an area that actually took final placement on my wish list of desirable locations. I was not too disappointed when the agent called to cancel. The owner's transfer had fallen through, and the listing had been taken off the market. During our conversation, and as any good agent would do, he offered to show me three other comparable listings in nearby buildings. As two of them were priced slightly higher than my budget allowed and

considering the location, I was hesitant. After all, I had just started in my search. But I was soon persuaded there would be no harm in taking a look.

The first listing I viewed was fine. It was actually not too bad. Carpeting I could live with, sans slippers. Freshly painted walls that were both crack and leak free. And I didn't need to leap over anything to get in the front door. In all honesty, it was an entirely decent place. Just kind of ho-hum. Nothing bad about it, but nothing too spectacular, either. I think that was it. Nothing about it moved me. Nothing that made me really, really, really want to live there. And considering the higher price tag attached, I didn't find the additional dollars involved a worthwhile investment.

But the next listing I viewed, golly! The next listing was "the one". I walked in and, "WOW!" The moment I stepped in the door I knew, this was it! Instead of cat, we were greeted by a beautiful arrangement of orchids on the hall table. From the door, the first thing that impressed me was the fabulous skyline view across the room. The main living area sported enough color and artwork to add interest and draw my attention in without overpowering. The furniture layout was open and comfortable. The kitchen's white-on-white color

scheme, something I would have personally never considered before, suddenly made me wonder how I could ever live without it! I envisioned myself in 3-inch Pradas™, (which I had never actually owned), preparing crème brulee and espresso for guests, (which I had never attempted before), while simultaneously charming everyone with my witty banter. (OK. That I've done.) How glamorous! When I got to the master bedroom, I couldn't help but notice, that fabulous skyline view was accessible from every window! Each room moved seamlessly into the next. And it was clean. Super clean. It even had a nice, clean smell! "I'll take it!"

While it didn't have the lake access, soaring ceilings, or square footage of the first condo. And it didn't have the fireplace, hardwood floors, or claw-foot tub of the second. And compared to the third listing I toured, it was nearly identical in price, location, size, and structural design, even mimicking a nearly identical skyline view. But this place was just sharp. It made me want to walk in and see more. And once I was in, it made me want to stick around. I could actually imagine how perfectly my furniture and accessories would look in this place. I could imagine myself living there. Though the condo itself was a more contemporary

structure than I might otherwise envisage, it had a quality that could easily adapt to anyone's style. While I literally raced through the previous listings I

toured, this place made me want to linger. I was there a full half hour at least, maybe longer. It was perfect.

As soon as I stepped out onto the street, I was on my cell phone with my mortgage guy. I told him what I found. I told him how much. I asked him to make it work. In less than 15 minutes, after some intense number crunching on his part, he called to discuss my options. If I put an additional $7,500 down, no problem! If I put another $5,000 down and economized from a car to a bicycle, I could swing it. If I put another $1,500 down and gave up the car, the bicycle, and food, I could just squeak by. I decided to try a combination of my last two options. I rationalized that by coming up with maybe something in between and downsizing my car for less substantial transportation, though preferably motorized, I could still afford the home of my dreams! I spent the rest of the afternoon trying to make it happen. I had a sit-down with my supervisor to find out how much I could get if I cashed out my 401K and company stock. I e-mailed a friend who had

once expressed interest in buying my old laptop and never-removed-from-the-box treadmill. I called my parents to find out if they had maybe forgotten to tell me about any savings accounts, government bonds, or other hidden assets issued to me as a kid that had since ballooned into my very own small, personal fortune by now. (FYI, the answer was a definite "no.")

Two frantic days later, I had pulled enough resources together to make an offer. But to my disappointment and as I had feared, another party had already beat me to the punch! And their offer was higher than mine. Not wanting to lose out on my dream home, I countered. A day later, I found I had been one-upped, again. Though I thought I had already reached my max, I miraculously managed to scrounge extra funding and padded my previous offer. I was on a mission! Who needs food? The agent was confident in my efforts. I was certain by sheer determination my labors would prevail. Which made losing out to the other buyer all the more difficult. I will spend the rest of my life knowing a complete and total stranger is living in my beautiful downtown condo, gazing out at my fabulous skyline views, and prancing around in their Pradas in my glamorous white-on-white kitchen. Heartbreaking.

But there are actually several great lessons to be learned about the power of staging your home in this story. To begin with, understand that like other buyers, in each given scenario I had a basic description of what I was going to be looking at. And like most

potential buyers, I was open enough to the possibilities. I made the effort, took the time, and took a look. I went out with buying in mind, and the opportunity to receive an offer was within reach for each prospective seller.

Secondly, if the owners of the first condo been suave enough to realize that by putting a little cash into fresh paint and new carpeting, and by fixing the crack and the leak, they likely would have been able to list for a higher price and easily receive an offer. Likewise, had the owners of the second condo taken cat out of the picture, along with about three fourths of the clutter, I wouldn't have missed the fireplace. I would have oohed and ahhed over the hardwood floors, and ditto with the claw-foot tub. I just couldn't see past all that muddle. I still remember the cat and the snow-globes more than anything else. In each case, the negatives far outweighed the positives. I walked into both with certain expectations. And it didn't take more than one quick peek to experience total disappointment.

Next, with regard to the third condo that was by all accounts nearly identical to "the one", its lack of pizzazz or ability to catch or hold my interest cost it a buyer. Had the effort been made to capture that "Wow!" factor, they could have easily been "the one". After all, I toured their listing first! The owners did not take their competition into consideration. That extra touch of zing made all the difference. It was like a slice of plain white cake without the icing vying for the same attention and compensation as its crème bruleé counterpart. What competition?

And finally, let's talk about the condo that warranted my offer. They did everything right. In fact, everything was so right, I was willing to jump through hoops to pay more. More than I originally planned to spend. More than the original asking price. They had a bidding war going on, simply based on their ability to present their product with style and flair, which resulted in a final sale that far exceeded the original list price.

"You are never given a second chance to make a good first impression!"

Need I say more?

CALIFORNIA RANCH

T

HIS CALIFORNIA RANCH

boasts hardwood floors on the main level, as well as two fireplaces and built-in bookshelves. With abundant knick-knacks, effects, and an unappealing furniture layout, these great features seemed to disappear within the jumbled confinement. At first glance, the eye took in all the trimmings, but struggled to focus on the structure's attributes. To help show-off the wonderful traits of this home, clutter was packed away and rooms were given a more considerate furniture arrangement. Within a few hours time, a house that seemed to have outgrown itself took on an entirely new personality. Attention was placed back on the home's exceptional focal points, resulting in a noticeably distinctive attitude.

THIS CALIFORNIA RANCH HAS
SEVERAL MAIN FLOOR ENTRIES,
WITH THE FRONT ENTRY LEADING
IMMEDIATELY INTO THE LIGHT-
FILLED LIVING ROOM.

AFTER The first step to staging this room was to box up the clutter and roll up the area rug. The sofa and loveseat were rearranged to give the floor plan a more open and inviting appeal. The new arrangement helps to frame the fireplace and subtly draw the eye in. While the back of the chair still faces the entry, it has inferior framework compared to the sofa. Angling its placement makes it even less prominent. And by pulling the chair into the room a full 18 inches, an actual entry was created and the living room defined. Artwork on the walls and heavy pink lamps and shades were exchanged for less obtrusive replacements that came from other areas of the house. Built-ins were arranged with a few brighter, heavier adornments to ensure a more concentrated view. Some of the shelving was purposely left empty to add to the open feel. To reduce distractions, the decorative screen and candle holders were removed from the hearth. Using bolder accessories on the mantle, artwork and a vintage shelf clock borrowed from a secondary upstairs room, along with a deep green arrangement of flowering eucalyptus, the fireplace now grabs attention at a glance.

BEFORE With the back of the sofa facing the entrance, the natural flow into the main living area was blocked. The room felt awkward and one-dimensional by leaving the center of the space empty and lining up accompanying furnishings along the wall. An area rug hid the beautiful wood floors beneath. The fireplace and built-ins had lost their impact as a focal point among the many little knick-knacks lining the mantle and shelving. Overall, the first view of this home's interior gave a buyer too much to look at and yet, nothing to really concentrate on.

AFTER A view of the living room from another position shows how the new arrangement compliments the area. By placing both the sofa and loveseat an entire 12 inches from the wall, the illusion of space is easily created, giving the room perspective. Without the area rug, the wood flooring now comes across as seamless. Removing the many diminutive knick-knacks previously strewn across the shelving and mantle in favor of a few distinct accessories makes all the difference in the room's initial influence.

"CLUTTER-BUG!"

CLUTTER IS THE NUMBER ONE SICKNESS FOUND IN MOST HOMES ON THE MARKET TODAY. Not at all surprising since we live in a "shop-'til-you-drop" society. Many of us, myself included, have a hard time resisting the temptation to indulge. But like my mom always says, "You can't keep hauling it in unless you start hauling it out, or eventually your house will explode!" (She really does say that.) And I'm pretty sure she's right. I've staged many homes that I'm convinced have already experienced the explosion or are certainly teetering on the brink. The dreaded clutter-bug is spreading in epidemic proportions! And one of the ugliest side effects is the overwhelming resistance to just let go. The feverish need to hang onto anything and everything ever found, purchased, passed along, or received as a gift. This symptom is frequently accompanied by the strong urge to display anything and everything ever found, purchased, passed along, or received as a gift. So, what do you do when you're faced with the unsightly reality of this house-crippling disease? While certainly not a cure-all, the quickest remedy is really quite pain free. Start packing!! Boxing up early is the best medicine. By doing so you'll easily relieve yourself of two ailments. Your house will show like the spacious, carefree space it was meant to be, and you will have gotten a jump start on your own relocation. Like yanking off a bandage, it's best to pull this off as quickly as possible. If you absolutely don't want to take something with you when you move, unload it now, but don't get too caught up in the process. This is definitely not the time to go tripping down memory lane. The more you procrastinate, the more this is going to seem like a chore, and you'll soon lose your motivation to finish. Once packed, store boxes in an out of the way corner of the basement, a secondary room, or the garage. Stack them neatly. If it is impossible to create complete order, cover the stack with a tarp or clean white sheet. Buyers are less likely to remember your temporary storage attempts as much as they will remember all the clutter. If you want to sort things out, wait until you get into your new place, and have time to go through each box thoroughly. And in the future always remember, "An ounce of prevention is worth a pound of cure."

AFTER This angle shows how the simplified layout plays up the space with a decisive intent. A spacious, uncluttered entry is a welcome invitation! Refined furnishings and accessories establish the comfortable setting and allow the buyer a chance to appreciate the view.

BEFORE In this view from the fireplace facing the front entry, the consequences of a poor furniture arrangement are even more apparent. Besides the back of the sofa obstructing passage and weighing down the room, the feeling was further amplified by the heavy presence of the glass cupboard and grandfather clock.

"Create an inviting appeal for buyers, the moment they step in the door."

IT IS IMPORTANT TO KEEP THE SPACE BETWEEN ADJOINING ROOMS VISUALLY APPEALING AND CONSISTENT TO HOLD THE BUYER'S INTEREST.

AFTER The grandfather clock was moved further down the wall for an added interest of height and weight to the dining room. By leaving some wall space unadorned and controlling select accessories, the buyer is given thoughtful direction to gently lead them from one room to the next.

AFTER From another perspective, the view from the living room to the stairway and dining room shows how flip-flopping the china cupboard with a smaller buffet from the opposite dining room wall makes a big difference. Adorned with a mirror the owner previously hung vertically atop the buffet adds to the airy mood. A wicker chair found unused in the basement contributes to a softer, more inviting appeal. With the new arrangement, wall space in the dining room was left unadorned to allow the eye a place to rest.

A STEP DIRECTLY INTO THE DINING
ROOM SHOWS THE BENEFITS OF
TRANSPOSING THE CHINA
CUPBOARD WITH THE BUFFET AND
THE RESOURCEFUL PLACEMENT OF
THE GRANDFATHER CLOCK.

BEFORE The dining room layout was very basic
and lacked pizzazz! Similar heights between the table
and buffet paired with monotonous white walls left this
room feeling one-dimensional.

AFTER With the bulk of the room
favoring the left, a more consistent feel is
achieved with this new arrangement.
Teaming the heavier china cupboard with
the table adds visual interest and breaks up
the wall space. The grandfather clock adds
balance to the room and helps to lead the
eye on. A hint of glamour was attained by
removing the table's protective cover and
polishing the wood. The resulting effect is a
warm, luminous reflection of light from the
overhead fixture and family room windows.
While the owner was hesitant to show off
the table top due to scratches and a little
warping, keep in mind that a buyer is there
to look at the house. They will be passing
through in a very short time. The advantage
of the added glow will far surpass any minor
flaws which will likely go unnoticed in a
home that is well staged.

AFTER   Another view, this time from the dining room to the living room, further validates the influence of a well thought-ou[t] plan. The weight of the room was shifted b[y] adjusting the distribution of heavy furnishings for balance. As a finishing touch, the taller floral arrangement on the dining room table was swapped out for a lower and fuller display. By intentionally disrupting the line between the table and the overhead light, recognition is placed directly on the stained-glass fixture, an added bonus for the buyer.

"*Thoughtful attention to detail is key to a well staged home.*"

THE SMALL KITCHEN HAS
WONDERFULLY BRIGHT WHITE
CUPBOARDS, APPLIANCES,
AND TRACK LIGHTING.

BEFORE The variety of coupons, clippings, and photos on the refrigerator and bulletin board distracted from the space. Scatter rugs further added to a cluttered feel.

AFTER Packing away the excess gives the kitchen a more expansive feeling. By simplifying the chaos, the focus is placed on the actual space. To keep the flooring open and consistent with the other rooms, rugs were removed. Tinfoil wrapped drip-pans on the stove were replaced for new. A bright bowl of fresh fruit adds a pop of color to the room.

BEFORE A variety of appliances, utensils, and other kitchenware made the countertops feel cramped and the space even smaller.

AFTER Only the absolute necessities remain on the counter for showings. And only the smallest rug from the set was left behind for the owner's comfort. When it comes to staging, especially kitchens, less is always more! The end result leaves this small kitchen feeling like workable space.

BEFORE With an oversized sectional crowding the entry to the sun room, this bright addition felt unapproachable. The confined arrangement, area rug, and untidy coffee table took away from the space and hid the warm oak floors. Adding to the dilemma, the large-screen television blocked the French windows and wonderful view of a poolside deck.

AFTER By splitting up the sectional into distinctive seating areas and removing the center component altogether, the room was expanded with very little effort. Moving the television to a family area on the second level helped accentuate this objective.

BEFORE A straightforward view gives a better understanding of how the television and fireplace vied for attention, with the television set the obvious winner. Throw blankets that beckoned the owners to sit and relax only strengthend the cluttered mood of this room.

AFTER While moving a heavier piece like this television set can seem like a lot of work to some, the resulting effect makes it a totally worthwhile endeavor. Clearing out the surplus and cleaning up the space made for an open and airy feel. The accent table between the windows is actually a jewelry chest brought in from the master bedroom and adorned with a small floral arrangement. Minimal accessories allow the eye to easily appreciate the fireplace.

STREAMLINED BEDDING AND ACCESSORIES MAKE THIS MASTER BEDROOM FEEL SPACIOUS AND RELAXING.

BEFORE The heavy waterbed in this room completely took over the space. Positioned on top of a large area rug and teamed with a brightly colored comforter and matching shams further accentuated the domination of this piece.

AFTER While moving the waterbed to pull up the rug beneath was indeed too much of an undertaking, simplifying the accessories helps achieve a lighter feel for this room. Busy bedding was replaced by an uncomplicated, creamy white quilt which is tucked neatly into the sides of the bed frame. Numerous photos displayed on and above the headboard were eliminated, creating a lighter mood between the substantial furniture piece and the rest of the room. A small doggie bed is hidden away in a nearby closet for showings.

Without any major moves of the main furnishings, an uncomplicated scheme is nevertheless achieved. Excess from the dresser, headboard, and floor was boxed and stored. A jewelry chest was moved to the family room where it was reinvented as an accent table. The 'new' bed covering is in reality a colorful patchwork quilt found in the owner's linen closet and reversed to expose the underside ticking. Disguised as shams on the bed pillows are two halves of a three yard fabric remnant purchased on clearance for just under $4. The material was ironed flat, folded like an envelope around the pillow form and secured with a safety pin to the back. These easy staging tricks are a cost-effective alternative to investing in new bedding. Accent pillows in more subdued tones assist in underscoring the massive bed. The two end sections of the dresser mirror were angled slightly inward, and the dresser was pulled six inches from the wall for depth. A fresh market bouquet of bright pink carnations makes a nice final touch.

BEFORE   From this angle, it is easy to see how attention was diverted from the space. The clutter and bedding were distracting and made the room feel smaller than its actual size.

KIDS' ROOMS ARE JUST THAT. THEY'RE KIDS' ROOMS! TO KEEP THEM IN ORDER FOR SHOWINGS, THE LESS THERE IS TO MESS, THE EASIER THEY ARE TO MAINTAIN.

BEFORE While buyers are typically forgiving of kids' rooms, it is still important to establish an eye-pleasing environment. This room was representative of many of the bedrooms found in homes with children.

AFTER The same staging rules apply when it comes to a child's bedroom. Nominal effects create a spacious and livable feeling. Stowing away the doll collection and stuffed toys helped put this room in focus. The dormer-turned-study was cleared out to emphasize this unique feature. While it isn't always easy keeping a child's room in check, by removing much of the clutter from the start, the effort to keep them looking sharp is minimized.

THE FAMILY ROOM WAS NICELY ARRANGED FOR THE SPACE. ALL THAT WAS NEEDED TO COMPLETE THE LOOK WAS A LITTLE CLUTTER CONTROL!

BEFORE Like a child's room, secondary rooms such as this upstairs family room are usually less important than main living areas. Though effort should always be made to keep a consistent flow from room to room.

▶

AFTER The only modification to this room was boxing up the clutter. While the change is not enormously significant, it is enough to make a noticeable difference and add impact.

CUSTOM DESIGN

THE PROPRIETORS OF TWO SHOPS, carrying both antiques and home décor, had this house custom designed to display their many collections. While the space originally fit their personal effects perfectly, as business flourished cherished items had no difficulty finding their way home. Over time, the once spacious layout soon turned into an exhibit of "must-haves." With so much furniture and so many collectibles to accommodate, the space just became smaller and smaller. To alleviate the over-stuffed feeling, excess was boxed and stored. Once spared down, a more appealing furniture layout was arranged to win back the roomy, expansive feel of the initial Custom Design.

AFTER The cluttered corner was simplified to show off the distinctive window. Christmas artwork was exchanged for something more seasonally appropriate. To open up the path to the living room, the table set was replaced by a comfortable chair. Removing ailing plants in favor of a bright green fern provides both color and life. The rug was pulled up to keep the flow clean and distraction-free.

BEFORE In the large foyer, a cluttered corner detracted from the unique window design. The over-grown cactus was straggly and unbecoming to the space. Holiday-themed artwork on the wall was out of season. A café set blocked the entrance into the living room. Like the cactus, a sickly ivy on the table was not a welcoming sign. The raggedy throw rug at the door made the space feel worn.

THE DRAMATIC EFFECT OF THIS LIVING ROOM SPACE WAS DIMINISHED BY THE HEAVY DECOR.

AFTER   To keep the room in context, accessories on the wall were downplayed. Vintage picnic baskets and the blue and white planters and vase are all from the owner's collections. The pictures are from the master bedroom. By using several significant but unfussy pieces, the new display created is proportionate to the room. One ledge was left purposely unadorned to enforce the simple appeal. The loveseat was pulled onto the far wall to open up the floor plan. Excess pieces were either stored or reinvented in other areas of the house. A full, lush plant was brought in to soften the space between the desk and the sofa. The new simple lines make the room appear larger, functional, and more inviting.

BEFORE   Looking from the entry to the living room, elaborate displays made the custom shelving feel like it was not actually part of the setting. While they are fixtures to be sold with the house and should be highlighted, they should not take over the wall or receive such negative attention! The effect of the overwhelming accessories amplified the uncomfortable bare wall space between the sofa and ledges by causing an exaggerated break in the eye-line view. Too much furniture and fillers resulted in an arrangement that blocked the dining room, making the area seem restricted.

AFTER An inventive plan gives the main living area a completely different feel! The new furniture layout exposes an open and easy flow. To give the room depth, the sofa was pulled 12 inches from the wall. Rather than storing the bulky trunk, previously located behind the loveseat, it is used as a side table. Lamp shades were updated to play down the vintage theme.

BEFORE A peek down to the living room from the loft above allowed a better understanding of the challenging arrangement below.

AFTER This view from the loft underscores how the clean lines play to the room!

THE LIVING ROOM FROM THE DINING ROOM POINT OF VIEW

AFTER The new layout compliments the view, both coming and going! When planning the arrangement of any space, especially important to an open floor plan such as this, every angle of the area should be taken into consideration. The room needs to be just as approachable on the way out as it is upon entry!

BEFORE From the dining room, this angle of the living room emphasized how muddled the layout was. The loveseat obstructed the space from both sides of the room. A closer look at the shelving shows how distracting the adornments were to the eye of the potential buyer.

"A well staged furniture arrangement should ensure a room feels spacious and ope from any point of view.

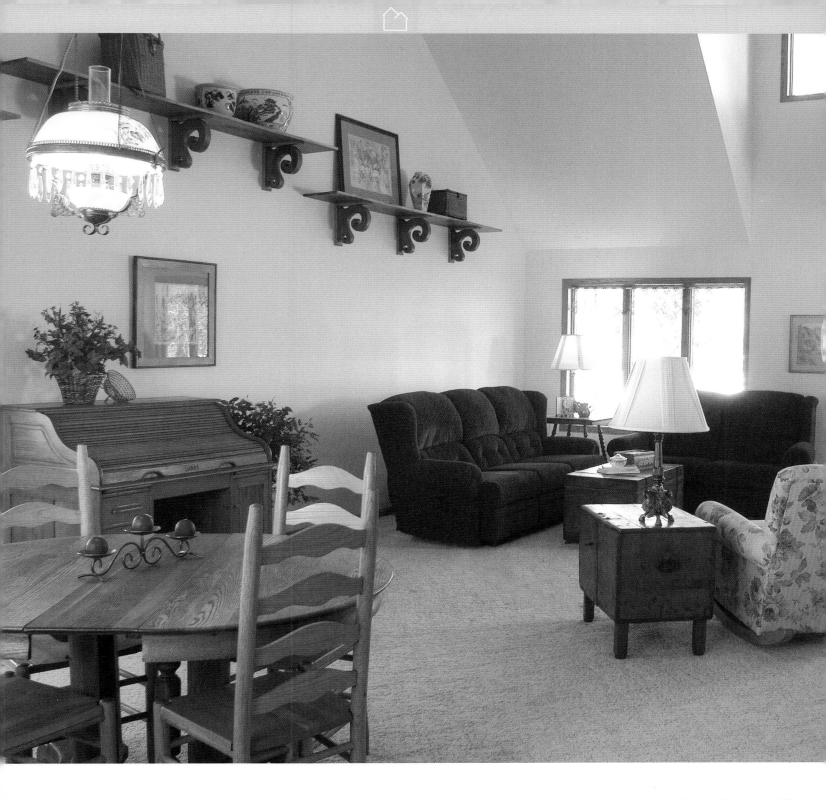

BEFORE Looking to the dining room from the living room, the tight space of the arrangement seemed out of sync with the open floor plan into the dining room. In contrast, too much on the walls made for a room that seemed overly decorated and heavy.

AFTER Removing all the plates and decorations from the walls automatically put the entire room back in focus. Rather than the eye following the line-up above the windows, the concentration is placed back on the space as a whole. The taller glass cupboard was placed in the corner, closer to the custom ledge, to lend to a more gradual procession up the soaring main wall. The rocking chair, previously sitting midpoint, was moved to the upstairs loft. A captains chair was pulled into the corner to balance the weight of the dining room. Chairs around the dining room table were angled for a more visually interesting space. From room to room, the generous size of the main floor living area is now apparent.

AFTER Another angle shows the buyer's viewpoint from within the room.

TOO MANY ACCESSORIES MUDDLE THE FLOW OF A ROOM AND TAKE THE BUYER'S EYE OFF THE ACTUAL SPACE.

AFTER As much as reasonably possible, frivolous adornments were stored. While it was not practical to move the larger pieces, removing less significant accessories modified the room's décor considerably. Notice, curtain toppers were left in place. By taking down the plate collection and leaving the ledge empty, it was easy to downplay their impact on the space. Through simple accessorizing and smart furniture placement, the personality of this dining room is much more appealing and positive.

BEFORE The loft view shows the entirety of the dining room. Old-world accessories, including a weather vane and spinning wheel, accentuated the antique theme of this home. A lace-edged tablecloth along with the window treatments, vintage handkerchiefs sewn together, added to the mood.

A WELL PLANNED KITCHEN WITH PLENTY OF STORAGE SPACE IS ALWAYS A WONDERFUL SELLING POINT.

AFTER To keep with the open and airy feel of this room, cupboards and countertops were edited to showcase minimal effects. By giving the space some breathing room, this kitchen was easily modified to show off the generosity of its original design.

BEFORE Like other rooms in this house, available space in the kitchen was used to display collections. Antique blue and white pottery, along with other vintage pieces, completely dominated the focus of the room.

"Box up significant groupings of any kind to show off the space, not your collections!"

"THE MAJORITY REPORT"

WHEN IT COMES TIME TO SHOW YOUR HOUSE FOR MARKET, THE MORE YOUR DÉCOR IS INFLUENCED ONE WAY OR ANOTHER, THE FEWER OPPORTUNITIES YOU WILL LIKELY ATTRACT. Not everyone has the same taste in style, and not everyone is going to love yours. This is one point many sellers just don't get. Suggesting they downplay their decorating is taken as a personal insult. What they fail to understand is that it has nothing to do with individual taste, and everything to do with how their decorating impacts the buyer's point of view. For instance, a home with strong, ultra-modern furnishings dressed in chrome and leather could be a big turn-off for someone who is not a fan of extreme contemporary. The space might feel cold to them and could easily sway their decision. Likewise, a buyer fiercely opposed to a country theme might not be able to see past the layers of chintz and plaid upholstery, but that is what they are going to see and that's what they will remember.

If your furnishings, artwork, or accessories are manipulating the concentration of your rooms, something needs to change. While it is unnecessary and unrealistic to replace your entire furnishings, modifying strong-handed decorating is a reasonable and attainable remedy. An ultra-modern scheme can be softened with touches of greenery, a few throw pillows to warm it up, and a more traditional piece or two scattered in the mix to detract from the sharp, contemporary edge. Altering a profoundly country décor by using patterns sparingly, editing furnishings, and minimizing adornments is usually enough to put the focus back on the space itself. So when it comes time to sell, think about what exactly you are trying to accomplish. Your house has become a product, and your goal is to appeal to the majority and increase your chances for an offer. A simple, pleasing mix that doesn't overpower is always the right solution. You never want your personal style to come between the house and a potential sale.

AFTER   To give the loft a tidy and fresh new look, clutter was boxed. Blankets were removed from the rail, allowing buyers the opportunity to take in the entire view. A set of table and chairs along with an oversized recliner were moved to basement storage to free up space. The aged sofa got a quick makeover with a slip cover found in the owner's linen closet. Pulling the sofa 18 inches from the banister produced the illusion of additional roominess and freedom to the space.

BEFORE This space felt cluttered and messy, with too much furniture lined along the perimeter and too many of the owner's personal effects laying around. The unique feature did not feel like the added bonus it should have been.

AFTER An artificial pine tree on the ledge, decorated each new season and permanently displayed, was warehoused in basement storage along with the recliner and bookshelf. A small side table was flip-flopped to the bedroom. Once excess was out of the way, the space took on a clean, basic appeal. The decorative table, previously utilized in the downstairs living room, was just the right size to fill corner space without overwhelming. For lighting, the same vintage table lamp was arranged with framed photos and silk greens to create an inviting but simple charm.

BEFORE From this viewpoint, it is easy to understand how the owners actually used this loft. While the arrangement made for a relaxing spot to read and watch television, it did little to stimulate the imagination of the potential buyer.

AFTER The closet and corner space were simplified. Detailing of woodwork above the closet is now apparent, and the window view is now accessible. A rocker from the living room and mirror from a secondary hallway were added to the setting. By making the area less complicated, buyers have an easier time envisioning their own effects in the space.

BEFORE The prominent sea of blue carpeting took over, as it was enforced by the bright pattern of the pillows, comforter, and strong artwork over the bed. Abrasive window treatments drew negative attention. Too much furniture lining the wall gave the space a flat, one-dimensional appearance. The display of antique talcum tins on top of the closet ledge hid the only element of oak detailing this room offered.

AFTER To tone down the intense blue carpeting, a new inexpensive comforter purchased on clearance for under $25 replaced the old one. The muted chartreuse background and understated blue hues tied the bedding and flooring together, while diminishing the stark contrast. The gap was closed further by flip-flopping the vivid artwork with two less substantial prints from the living room, breaking up the strong influence of blue. Adding to the tranquil feel, sheer nylon fabric purchased for $1 per yard was cut into equal sections and draped over the tension rods in the windows to soften the effect. By sliding one nightstand 24 inches from the bed and replacing the other with the small side table from the loft, bare wall was allowed to show through enhancing the airy illusion of the space. As a final touch, solid colored pillows in lighter blue and green tones and a bud vase with silk lilac stems pull the scheme together.

AFTER   Eliminating one dresser and packing away the hat box collection and adornments opened up the space. The club chair was brought into the room, away from the window. Slanting it off the wall and adding a floor lamp found in storage created a cozy reading area. The new arrangement adds both interest and functionality to the layout. Softer window treatments allow natural lighting to flood the room. Accessories used in moderation, including a larger arrangement of silk lilac stems, help to tone down the blue of the carpeting. The new look is relaxing, less muddled, and complimentary to the space.

BEFORE   From this angle, the furniture and layout of the room looked monotonous. On the far wall, dual dressers and a stack of antique hat boxes directed the eye. Too many knick-knacks make the space feel cluttered. Unflattering window treatments were distracting and blocked light. And a club chair stuffed in the corner made approachability to the window views difficult.

THIS SPACIOUS BATH HOLDS
AN ABUNDANCE OF
DESIRABLE FEATURES.

AFTER   To play to the opulence of this space, rugs were removed to show off the glowing floor covering. Lush green plants were brought in to add color and enhance the feeling of luxury and indulgence. A basket with rolled hand towels and extravagant soaps add to the pampered ambiance. Through simple accessorizing, the master bath turned into an inviting oasis.

BEFORE   A master bathroom offering double sinks, a whirlpool tub, and separate shower stall did not receive the attention it deserved. Sparkling floors were hidden beneath bath mats, breaking up the flow of the design.

URBAN CONDO

AN EFFICIENT URBAN CONDO made for a fine bachelor pad, sporting both ample storage and living space. But when the previously single owner committed to couple-hood, merging furniture and effects combined with robust color choices made this compact dwelling seem to explode! With a baby now on the way, the only option was to place this one-bedroom on the market. Two gallons of primer and four gallons of fresh paint later, a minor facelift made a major impact on rebellious rooms. By toning down the color on the walls and rethinking the furniture layout, a listing that once overpowered was easily transformed into sleek, streamlined space with truly urban appeal.

THE HALLWAY IS THE BUYER'S
FIRST VIEW INTO THIS
SMALL CONDO.

BEFORE With the front door opening
directly into a hallway, this space needed a
number of changes in order to create a positive
first impression. Using multi-primary colors on
opposing walls chopped up the space giving it a
restricted feel. And by taking on double-duty as
a resting spot for an unused card table and
chairs, the already confined condo gave the
impression that storage was limited. With so
much attention directed at the color, the built-in
office area and closets to the left were virtually
unnoticeable compared to the intense backdrop.

AFTER By washing the walls in a much less complicated color scheme, the space was tamed by a light shade of taupe called Maisen Blanc by Hirshfield's Paint and Wallcovering. The new hue lifts the hallway space while simultaneously flattering the wood floors and downplaying the conflicting wall angles. Leaving the door open at the end of the path gives a peek into the rooms beyond and serves to add to an expansive feeling. By neutralizing the colors and adding the laptop, a once invisible built-in workspace is now noticeably defined.

TO THE IMMEDIATE RIGHT OF THE ENTRY HALL, THE NATURAL MOVEMENT OF THE BUYER WOULD FLOW STRAIGHT INTO THE KITCHEN.

BEFORE The kitchen is a good size for the dimensions of the condo, but it was confining with the muddled decor. Between the white throw rug and the high sheen of the two-tone paint scheme on the cupboards, the marble floors were completely overlooked. Likewise, the combination of clutter on and above the cupboards, an over-sized microwave and stand, director's chair, T.V. trays, and red walls would baffle the eye of the buyer. An old, broken light fixture over the table added to the dated feeling.

AFTER By continuing the hallway color into the kitchen, a nice even flow is created. Repainting the cupboards in Almond by Hirshfield's Paint and Wallcovering created a clean line. Using a softer paint color on the cupboards with an eggshell finish and removing the rug altogether helps illuminate the beautiful marble floors. Once excess effects were cleared from the eating area, mahogany cabinets were borrowed from the living room and reinvented to help balance out the weight of the marble and add a sense of depth to the room. As a final touch, the broken and dated lighting fixture was replaced with an inexpensive lighted paper lantern in a cheery spring green. The overall ambiance of the kitchen is now sleek and elegant.

AFTER With a thoughtful color scheme and minimal accessories, the eye is now drawn in. The focus has been taken off the chaos and replaced with a spacious sense of care-free order. By establishing a stylish and refined space, the buyer is now free to appreciate all this kitchen has to offer.

BEFORE An opposite view of the kitchen accentuates the need to simplify. The color choices alone were vastly responsible for how this space was perceived. Teamed with too much clutter, the entire room seemed unruly with no distinct focal points.

"*Soft colors make a small room feel spacious!*"

"THE WALLFLOWERS"

A few years ago while choosing paint colors for my first home, I was instantly drawn to a fiery shade of salmon! At a time when the "it" look of the moment was "anything-as-long-as-it's-white," this vibrant, totally original color seemed just the right expression of individuality I was looking for. I quickly purchased several gallons of the stuff on behalf of my living room. Happily I will admit, I felt like quite the rebel when I got home and started smearing it on the walls. In my mind, I compared the act itself to spray painting graffiti on a public building. It felt both dangerous and incredibly decadent! By 2 a.m. I had finished the job and decided to call it a night. But within a few hours I was more than anxious to inspect my handiwork by the first light of day. As I hurried out of my bedroom, I was confronted by a shocking surprise! The color that seemed so rich and seductive the night before had mysteriously morphed itself sometime between 2 a.m. and 8 a.m. It was pink! I mean, really pink!! The kind of pink that can only be found in a bottle of Pepto-Bismol™. I was mortified.

My first visitor, a friend who stopped by later in the day, made a witty observation. "Well, it's definitely pink!" Feeling humiliated and now a little defensive, I was quick to correct him, "It's not pink! It's salmon!" The on-going reaction of other guests varied from, "Wow! I love it." to my best friend's rather forthright remark, "What on earth were you thinking?" As days and weeks passed and the initial shock began to wear off, the color actually started to grow on me. Throwing caution to the wind, I decided to go for it. Diligently, I arranged furniture and hung pictures, artwork, and window treatments. By the time I was finished it had turned into a space I genuinely liked, though my controversial paint choice continued to receive mixed reviews from family and friends.

Eventually, as my style and furnishings evolved, I repainted in a soft mocha. While hints of my former, albeit ill-fated affair with the vivacious salmon hue lingered, I toned it down considerably. Through painful editing I allowed myself only a few remaining glimpses into the room's formidable past. In the end, I kept the brightly colored throw-pillows around along with some of the artwork and accessories for accent. Leftover paint from the original scheme, of which I still had plenty, took on a new life when smoothed over bathroom walls. The color that had once offended and dominated my living room was far more striking in a smaller dose. With the transformation complete, the difference was amazing! Everyone loved it, not just a few. Even those who had previously complimented my décor admitted to liking the makeover even more. So much so, several used the identical mocha palate in their own homes, teaming it with bright shots of green or deep blues, or blending it with paler neutrals and white. How flattering!

We all have different tastes in style. And if you can't express yourself in your own home, then where? But when it comes time to sell, your choices may drastically affect your prospects and become significantly more important. The reality is, color makes a statement. And the stronger the color, the stronger the statement. The entire message you want to communicate to the buyer is, "Look at this wonderful house!" not, "Check out my bright salmon walls!" I frequently hear the argument, "If the new owner wants to paint over it, let them paint over it!" Which they may certainly do regardless. But it should be a personal choice on their part, if and when they decide to buy your house, not a decision they've been forced to consider beforehand. They may very well make the decision not to consider it at all and simply move on to the next listing. While one or two secondary rooms sporting stronger paint colors are usually not a "make-it-or-break-it" for most buyers, main living areas with bold colors of paint are. If your walls are making any kind of daring statements on their own, you will be doing yourself an enormous favor by repainting them.

When choosing a new color for this purpose, it is best to stick with impartial tones. Paler, neutral shades fair far better in real estate marketing for the simple fact that they are much less personal and easily conform to any décor. Anything with a yellow undertone, such as tan or linen, is typically a good choice. Even a pale shade of beige is preferred, though. I usually recommend steering clear of colors with a heavy pink undertone. The same goes for anything with a hint of blue or gray. My reasoning is pretty simple. Not only do yellow tones warm the room, but as a rule, it is easier for someone with predominately red, blue, or gray furnishings to work with yellow undertones. Much tougher for someone with furnishings in earthier tones to work with walls that may strongly suggest hues in pink, blue, or gray.

My friends reacted positively to the new, muted palate of my living room, because it was a color they could all relate to. It made them feel comfortable. And they were not overwhelmed when they walked in the door. That's the same affect your walls should have on potential buyers. Choose a simple color scheme anyone can live with!

BEFORE From the kitchen, the view into the main living area was again weighed down by the strong influence of color. An unfavorable furniture arrangement underscored the expansive mustard walls. While the vaulted ceiling definitely commanded attention, it seemed to be its own entity making the top half of the room feel out of sync with the rest. The stark wood beam further exaggerated the disproportionate space.

WITH INTENSE WALL COLORS WELL HIDDEN BENEATH A SOFT BLANKET OF TAUPE, THIS ROOM AUTOMATICALLY TOOK ON A SUBDUED AND EVEN-TEMPERED AURA.

AFTER The wood beam was painted white to help it blend. To create the same subtle consistency from one room to the next, the rug was removed producing a more uniform effect. The mahogany cabinets were emptied and moved to the kitchen. The five-drawer dresser was flip-flopped with its oversized counterpart in the bedroom. By pulling furnishings from the wall, an open and more interesting layout is the result.

Painting the same, subtle color from the hallway, to the kitchen, to the main living area of this condo creates a soothing background for this small space.

AFTER A fresh paint color and a more open layout adds to the new, spacious ambiance of this room. The rug was rolled up and moved into storage. Bookcases were cleaned out and moved to the kitchen. The small chest of drawers was flip-flopped with a large dresser from the bedroom. This exchange serves two purposes. The smaller piece took up less space in the bedroom, and the mahogany dresser took on a new roll in the living room and added contrast and bulk to even out the composition. After freeing up space in the closets, the computer cart was rolled out of sight. The speakers, which were not connected, were banished to storage. Accessories were kept to a bare minimum, adding to the streamlined effect.

BEFORE From another view of the living room, it is easy to see how murky and congested the layout of this room seemed. A sofa, with its back to the main entry, blocked the natural flow of traffic into the room. The line-up of furnishings along the wall, combined with the extreme paint choices, made the space seem to close in on itself. Likewise, a dark area rug and too much clutter added to the heavy feeling.

BEFORE From this side of the room, the space had too much going on to produce a nice, easy flow. The powerful color on the walls felt shocking in the small confinement and took attention away from the actual structure. A jumbled arrangement made the room feel cramped and uninviting.

AFTER The view toward the kitchen shows how open the flow now feels. Through simple design and consideration, the motivation of this setting has changed dramatically. With only two shared windows in the conjoining rooms, the curtains and hardware were removed to put them in focus. Adorning the top of the reinvented dresser, two vases in brighter, multi-shades of green, mimic the new light fixture in the kitchen. An inexpensive purchase, they add a nice pop of color and help accentuate the view into the eating area. By removing the rug, it is easy to see how the wood flooring has turned into a great selling point.

THE BUILT-IN OFFICE.

AFTER ▶ A close look at the built-in office space shows how user friendly it becomes when dressed down in softer colors and by boxing up the book clutter. Shelves were accessorized with bright vases and framed artwork, playing to the space without overwhelming.

THE BATHROOM.

AFTER ▶ With a bathroom view directly off the living room, it is important to keep the scheme of this condo consistent through color. To emphasize the uniformity from one room to the next, the woodwork within was painted white. Taking that one step further, the steel-blue shower curtain was replaced by a vivid rendition in white and shades of green to draw the eye in.

THE CLOSETS.

BEFORE   The closets in the living room were over-stuffed and messy. Since they are the main source of storage in this home, the closets took on additional importance.

AFTER By removing the owner's effects completely, save for absolute bare necessities, the idea of spaciousness is conveyed. It is extremely important to make sure closets, especially when they are so vital to the room you are staging, are cleaned out. Closets located in entryways, master bedrooms, kitchens, and designated linen closets are typically those that catch a quick peek from buyers. Take some extra time to make sure they are just as well presented as the rest of your home.

FROM THE BATH AREA, THE FLOOR PLAN MOVES TO THE BEDROOM.

AFTER Painting the walls a soft gold provides a nice, warm glow and makes for a subtle transition into the bedroom. In this case, replacing the carpeting was a good investment. The television bracket, which the owners planned to take with them, was removed, as should any fixed effects that are not being sold with the home. By storing the excess, clearing out the mess under the bed, and adding a coordinating fitted sheet to the box spring, the room was given a neater appearance and seems much more inviting.

BEFORE The painted stripes on the walls did nothing for this room but mistakenly play-up the worn carpeting. Too much excess, the untidy clutter under the bed, and exposed box spring made the room feel generally unappealing.

"While many sellers opt to give the buyer a 'carpeting allowance,' it is always a much better choice and worthwhile effort to replace worn or dated flooring before the house goes to market. Not only does it make for a better presentation, it also projects the sentiment of a home that has been well cared for. And by alleviating the buyer of the responsibility to replace, you have given them one less reason to reject!"

AFTER A closer look shows how the uncluttered corner gives access to the closets. Moving the nightstand one foot from the bed helps boost the feeling of roominess by exposing some of the bare wall from one piece to the next. The painted canvas in warm shades of orange and brown, a flea market find, adds to the warmth of the room.

BEFORE From another angle, the changing table in the corner for the expected new addition was taken to storage to free up the much needed space.

TRADITIONAL

TUDOR

HILE THE FURNISHINGS matched the style of this five bedroom Tudor, it lacked the self-confidence to stand up for itself and command attention! Wood paneling and trim abound throughout, which is a typical feature in this type of traditionally styled home. But the dark undertones cast a shadow on the way it presented itself to potential buyers. What should have been major selling points turned into drawbacks. Through a little thoughtful rearranging, a few "tricks of the trade," and a minimal investment from the homeowner, the dreary state of mind adapted by this established family home took a turn for the better!

THE FIRST VIEW FROM THE
DOORWAY OF THIS HOME LEADS
INTO A SMALL FOYER FEATURING
OAK PANELING, AN OAK
STAIRCASE, AND ITALIAN TILES.

BEFORE The eye is directly drawn to the
decorative area rug, which not only hid the flooring
but broke up the space as well. The chair and
console seem to exaggerate a bottom-heavy
appearance. And too much exposed paneling
combined with the oak banister made this foyer
feel like it was suffocating in woodwork.

AFTER Carefully chosen accessories put an end to several dilemmas. An image framed in green and gold which was borrowed from the upstairs hallway, a bright silk fern, and a gold buffet lamp help to resolve many issues. By adding warmth and interest to the console top and removing the colorful rug, the line of view is now brought to eye level. The contrast of the accessories against the paneling assists in breaking up the woodwork and helps to enhance the effect, rather than overwhelm it. With the addition of the buffet lamp, the hallway light was purposely turned off to frame the paneled wall and add a touch of drama. A prospective buyer is now able to see the inviting dignity of this foyer, making the first impression a positive one.

BEFORE From another point of view, you can see how congested the corner of this staircase appeared. Too many obstacles interrupted the flow of the space. There was a lack of distinction between stairway, chair, console, and paneling. The spindles of the chair competed with the spindles of the banister. At first glance, the eye tended to get lost in the gridlock.

AFTER It is easy to understand how this foyer benefits by eliminating the chair and rolling up the rug. Removing the chair not only liberates the space of one less barrier, it exposes the metal grating of the console to add contrast. The bare floor instantly adds a feeling of freedom and offers a smoother transition to the next room. Considerate accessorizing encourages a subtle glimpse up the staircase. The overall result ensures an easy visual journey from one room to the next.

THE FORMAL DINING ROOM, DIRECTLY OFF THE FOYER, FEATURES OAK CEILING PANELS AND A VINTAGE CHANDELIER.

BEFORE The combination of low-light windows and the teal colored carpeting did not mingle well in this room. While the mirror hanging above the buffet echoed light, the lack of illumination left it nothing to reflect. The pale linen tablecloth which had been placed there to brighten the room only served to draw attention to the table. Too many chairs made movement around the table a tight squeeze.

AFTER As a result of leaving the chandelier and buffet lamps on, the room receives a jolt of much needed light which automatically reflects in the mirror, making it all the more constructive. Removing the tablecloth uncovers another shiny surface to emulate the rays, providing an all-over warm glow to the room. The captains chairs, at the head of the table and opposite, were ordered to their neutral corners to free up walking space around the table. An arrangement of silk flora and greenery adds a soft touch of color and elegance to the overall display. With these few simple changes, the line of view is easily directed around the room. By consciously drawing attention to the features of the paneled ceiling and vintage lighting fixture, the entire dining room inadvertently received a quick face-lift.

THE MORE SPACIOUS A
KITCHEN APPEARS, THE MORE
IT WILL IMPRESS.

AFTER By packing away the unnecessary, countertops take on an even more spacious appearance. The coffee maker was left behind for being the only appliance actually used on a daily basis. Other items on display are purely decorative and used strategically to keep the line of view moving around the kitchen. A similarly efficient attitude was carried into the eating area for consistency. The candelabra, which felt too close in proximity to the decorative lighting fixture, was replaced by a less substantial centerpiece. The ornate metal bowl and small bunch of ivy, which had been previously displayed in the dining room, does not detract from the hanging fixture like the candles did. Even chair cushions were pulled to keep the look clean. The changes seem almost minute, but examine the before and after closely and consider the difference in presentation.

BEFORE While the kitchen in this home was actually quite well cleared, the countertops still boasted a little too much clutter for showings. The less counter space there is to work with, the more that needs to appear available. Several low-use appliances and carry-alls for newspapers, magazines, and mail took up too much room.

FROM THE KITCHEN, THE VIEW INTO THE ADJOINING FAMILY ROOM BOASTS A WOOD-BURNING FIREPLACE WITH OAK MANTLE, OAK WOODWORK, AND PANELED CEILING

BEFORE A dowdy furniture layout and lack of definition did nothing to play up the room's features. The russet upholstery on the chair not only blocked the path to the windows, the sharp contrast of color open competed for attention that should unequivocally go directly to the fireplace. By mimicking the woodwork and ceiling panels, the coffee table also added to foiling the rooms objective.

AFTER Taking the chair out of the picture draws the attention to the fireplace. In its absence, the path to the window is also much more accessible. Pulling the sofa a full 24 inches from the window not only takes the fireplace into consideration, it allows the potential buyer to get a closer look at the scene in the backyard. By flip-flopping the coffee tables with a glass and powdered-iron version from the living room, the distinction of materials adds new appreciation to the room's oak features. A transparent tabletop also helps to lighten up the room. Over the mantle, decorative vases and greens help to soften the painting rather than making it a focal point on its own. The silk ficus tree, previously situated in an unflattering corner of the family room, was repositioned to bring some variance in height to the setting. An assortment of greenery also cheers up the space. A dish of hard candies on the coffee table is an invitation for visiting realtors and their clients to stop, linger, and enjoy the view.

TREAT THEM RIGHT!

ONCE THEY HAVE COMPLETED TOURING A HOME WITH THEIR CLIENT, IT IS CUSTOMARY FOR A VISITING REALTOR TO LEAVE A BUSINESS CARD BEHIND. Typically, the card is handed off as a final thought upon leaving on a table or countertop somewhere convenient to the front door. Rather than following suit, a great way to differentiate your house from other listings is by controlling the drop off area. Pick the spot within your house you feel most worthy of a second look. An area that boasts some type of outstanding selling point or a central location with an overall view both make good choices. Display an attractive dish filled with foil-wrapped hard candies along with a few of your realtor's business cards somewhere within your chosen setting. This will alert the visiting agent that this is where they are to leave their business card. It will also signify to them, and more importantly to their client, the candied treats are for their enjoyment. A thoughtful gesture on its own, this small effort will play out to your advantage. By gently forcing the agent to return with potential buyer in tow or persuading them to stop and linger as they are touring, they will be spending extra time in your home. Prolonging their visit in this positive manner will automatically increase your chance to impress, and you are more likely to be remembered.

BEFORE The same room from another viewpoint shows how it connects to the living room via French doors. Again, the russet upholstery nabbed too much attention in an opposing corner. Note how the chair in front of the rails also offended the path of movement in the other direction. The hassock lended to the confusion by visually connecting the fireplace to the television cabinet, making it appear to be one component rather than distinguishing the fireplace. Closed doors gave the room bad karma by sealing off potential buyers from the rest of the house. A small cluster of family photos and greeting cards was an invitation to snoop.

AFTER The pale yellow chairs were flip-flopped from the living room to both lighten up the space and take the focus off the furniture. Notice how the exchange of chairs and coffee table also places the emphasis back on both the woodwork and paneled ceilings. Removing the hassock helped turn the fireplace into its own, well-defined element. One French door is left purposely closed to accentuate awareness of yet another wonderful attribute. One is left open to give the potential buyer a hint into the next room and offer them a welcoming sign to further explore.

By arranging the chairs together, a secondary conversational area was created to give the room a more user-friendly feel.

THE FURNISHINGS IN THIS TRADITIONAL LIVING ROOM WERE FLIP-FLOPPED TO ENHANCE THE SPACE.

AFTER Flip-flopping the coffee table and chairs from this room to the family room next door is an enormous benefit to both. The lack of wood paneling on the walls and neutral carpet is better suited to handle the stronger upholstery colors. The darker wood table serves to anchor the arrangement. By moving the side table out of the corner and giving it a new home under the artwork, a more well-rounded space results. Just as lightening up the family room helps accentuate the paneled ceilings, the darker colors add weight to this room and creates a balance between the ceiling and floor. Pulling the sofa eight inches from the wall adds depth. An interesting display tones down the wood coffee table.

BEFORE The white carpeting and south-facing windows in the living room made a nice, neutral setting. But compared to the rest of the rooms on the main floor, it felt surprisingly stark in contrast. While the paneled ceiling was definitely noticeable, it felt as if it were closing in. Too many elements stuffed in the back corner and too much white space between the artwork and small accent table below left this room feeling out of sync.

AFTER   Adding an additional wing back chair relocated from the upstairs master bedroom balances the stronger colors on both sides of the room. The deep red upholstery warms the cold walls. Heavier elements of wood create more stability in movement from one room to the next.

BEFORE   The view from the living room to the foyer helps to show the division in consistency this room had with the rest of the house. Compared to the heavy use of oak throughout, the white walls felt out of place and made the room feel empty and cold in comparison. A hibernating shrub lent itself to the stark mood.

"Thoughtful furniture placement can greatly enhance a room's features and downplay its shortcomings!"

FLIP-FLOPPING!

FOR LACK OF A BETTER TERM, FLIP-FLOPPING IS ESSENTIALLY EXCHANGING FURNISHINGS OR ACCESSORIES FROM ONE ROOM TO ANOTHER. Not an idea most homeowners easily see as an alternative to resolve their dilemmas. People get used to the way they use a room. They become accustomed to the function of their furnishings. It is hard to see past that. Even at my suggestion, I have run into resistance. "This chair is casual. That room is formal." "But the pieces came together as a set. They can't be broken up." "Aren't people going to notice it's a dresser, not a buffet?" Keep in mind that a potential buyer is not there to inspect your furniture. The entire point of staging your home is to show off the house itself. It is likely that whatever is ailing will draw even more attention than whatever flip-flopping you do to fix it. And it is just as likely, that attention is going to be negative. Potential buyers have no idea how one piece or another came into your possession or why. They are not aware you bought those tables to go with that sofa or you are using chairs from your dining room to fill an empty corner in your living room. If you need space in the bedroom and your dining room has more space than it can handle, why can't you turn your dresser into a buffet? Who's going to know? It might be a little inconvenient to fetch clean socks in the morning, but the condition is temporary. Adjust your life around it and consider the outcome of your sacrifice. Flip-flopping can resolve many issues resulting in a perfect presentation. And a perfect presentation is exactly what you want!

BEFORE The master bedroom is quite well sized, but felt confined because of excess furniture. A small sofa closed off the path to the windows, and an oversized family portrait surrounded by smaller framed photos put the emphasis on the life of the homeowner.

AFTER Removing the sofa to a spare room and the side-chest to downstairs storage opened up the space significantly. The family portrait went to join the sofa and was replaced by a vintage mirror. A chair, previously found in the foyer, replaced the sofa, and the table and silk flower arrangement were brought over from another corner of the room. To bring in a splash of color, the dresser was enhanced with a bouquet of silk flowers arranged in a vase the owners already had. To draw attention to the windows, a twin to the picture used in the foyer was hung near by.

BEFORE The dressing area of the master bedroom felt cramped. The heavy wardrobe, wing back chair, covered dressing table, and occasional table were simply too much to make this space feel useful. Between the chair and the basket of magazines, the door to the walk-in closet felt off limits.

AFTER To free up this dressing space, everything but the wardrobe was relocated or placed in basement storage. The wing back chair was used in the living room. The occasional table accompanied the side chair to the opposite side of the room, creating a cozy reading spot. The matching chair was part of a set, discovered when moving other pieces to storage. Its slight demeanor made it the perfect accent. By opening up the space and leaving the mirror in place, a functional dressing area has been defined.

BEFORE Besides a storage room, the lower level of this home held another wonderful surprise, a finished family room and bedroom, complete with private bath accommodations. With no furniture to fill the space, the area was used for storage overflow.

AFTER Boxes and leftovers were reorganized to fit into storage. Using extra furnishings from around the house and a patio set, the main area was set up to show the possibilities of this room to prospective buyers.

AFTER This bedroom, created out of mismatched pieces found around the house, was easily transformed into livable space with very little effort. The more finished a house looks, the more appealing it will be to the potential buyer.

"*Never* leave a buyer trying to guess the function of a room. Always show them livable space!"

COUNTRY
FARMHOUSE

AN 1890'S FARMHOUSE

with a 1990's facelift gave this home a real country feel, appropriate to the owner's décor and a rural lifestyle. The strong use of color, paint scheme, and wall covering were left untouched to show that even slight differences make an impact on a home's first impression. By playing down the whimsy, standardizing the accessories, and opening up the furniture arrangement, this Country Farmhouse is now open to the possibilities!

A COUNTRY KITCHEN IS THE FIRST IMPRESSION A BUYER WILL HAVE OF THIS HOME AS THEY WALK IN THE DOOR!

BEFORE With a front entrance leading directly into the kitchen, it is equally as important to create a welcoming environment as if this room were a grand foyer!

AFTER To create an inviting atmosphere without going overboard, and to downplay the country scheme, many of the accessories were packed up and boxed. By reducing the number of whimsical touches, a more universal appeal was established. The bowl of apples on the counter was an easy, inexpensive, and edible way to bring a touch of color to the room. A few of the apples were even placed on the window sill and rolled across the countertop to strengthen their impact.

BEFORE The view from the other side of the kitchen looking towards the main entrance showed how the line up of effects along the ceiling kept the focus at the top of the cupboards.

AFTER From the dining room, here is a look at the full impact of the kitchen. While it was not necessary to make major changes, a few easy steps transformed the concentration of this room dramatically.

AFTER To bring the buyer's eye into the entire kitchen, the continuous display on the top of the cupboards was simplified. Purposely grouping several larger arrangements and leaving some of the open wall show through helped to break up the space. By using a few stronger effects on the countertops, including the mixer and fruit bowl, a balance has been established. Rather than leading the eye directly to the top of the cupboards, the buyer is now free to take in all the room has to offer.

THIS FORMAL DINING ROOM BOASTS SHINY WOOD FLOORS AND A WONDERFUL BUILT-IN GLASS CUPBOARD.

AFTER   Removing furnishings is not always an option. But by toning down the effects, it was not necessary. After packing up most of the ornamentation, a cleaner look gave the space a more open feel. Clearing out the glass cupboard exposed more of the oak woodwork helping to downplay the wallpaper.

BEFORE   The busy print in the dining room and a burgundy painted ceiling are an overpowering combination with the mix of antique furnishings and accessories, giving this space a very distinct flavor. Table runners and crocheted adornments added to the country feel of this room.

"To tone down busy wallcovering, use accessories sparingly."

BEFORE Another view into the dining room shows how the wallpaper captured the eye's attention. A burgundy scarf hung over the window further dramatized the printed walls and heavy ceiling color.

AFTER To soften the color scheme of this room, the window treatment was simply removed. An easy approach to breaking up the wall covering was to pull a vintage display case off a side partition and place it on a more prominent wall. Not only does this serve to cover some of the print, it also adds a nice variation of height and wood finish to the all oak room. A rocking chair was brought in from the adjoining living room for stability. The area rug in this case was left in place. By acting as a buffer between the oak dining set and oak floors, a balance was created. Its small size and strong color help to keep the room in focus. Without it, the eye would be drawn up to the dark painted ceiling. As a final touch, a colorful bouquet and bright green plant both help to keep the basic scheme from taking over.

THE LIVING ROOM FROM THE DINING ROOM POINT OF VIEW

AFTER A more distinctive furniture arrangement helps to ease up the sedate impression of the room. By drawing the sofa and loveseat closer into the space, the stark open area of vacant floor is interrupted. To play to the fireplace, the new arrangement purposely frames the hearth, drawing the eye in. Moving the sofa from the wall allows visitors a close-up chance to glimpse at the scenery outside and also adds to a more spacious feel. To enhance this effect, the rocking chair was moved to the dining room and several of the extra furnishings were placed in basement storage, along with the heavy artwork and wreath. The wall next to the window is left bare, and a brighter print framed in gold helps to put attention back on the fireplace and lighten up the room.

BEFORE The first peek into the living room showed how the darker paint colors cast a shadow over this space. With a line-up of furnishings on the wall, the much exposed carpeting further added to the lopsided weight of the room. A forest green sofa set and a few too many chairs created a heavy, cluttered feel. A dreary wreath of dried greens over the mantle added to the foreboding atmosphere. Artwork in shades of deep blue and gray further overcast the space.

AFTER The vintage piano, a cumbersome piece that did not move easily, was pulled far enough down the wall to be set at an angle for the sake of space. By pulling the loveseat into the room, a walkway was left behind the piece to allow access and create depth to the space. A chair next to the piano was placed for the convenience of the children's music teacher. To lighten the room, a gold framed picture was turned into a grouping between the angles of the chair and piano. A floor lamp was brought in from another room to bring in light. Though the colors are still dark, the room feels more in sync with itself and gives the buyer a better idea of space usage.

BEFORE To the right of the living room, the same dilemma was apparent. Darkly painted walls with a vacant space in the middle of the room, especially noticeable with the lighter flooring, only enhanced the predicament. With pieces lined up on the rooms perimeter, the space felt awkward and out of balance.

"SPARE CHANGE"

ONE OF MY ALL-TIME FAVORITE LINES WAS DELIVERED IN THE WOODY ALLEN FILM, "MIGHTY APHRODITE." The wife of Allen's character is talking to her mother regarding a relocation they are contemplating. Asked when they are going to make the move, the wife says, "Oh mother, we don't want to get into that discussion. Because, you know, I think we should move, and Lenny is a devoted upper-east sider, or shall I say, is opposed to change in any form?" It always makes me laugh, because I know so many people this statement could apply to.

I once had a client with a really great house in a really great neighborhood. The yard was beautifully landscaped, and from the outside, it was pretty spectacular. Several offers had already been made, all well below a very fair list price, and none of which had been accepted. After six months on the market, both homeowner and agent were perplexed. But what I found when I stepped inside was an over decorated mish-mosh of distractions, and it was obvious to me why the house hadn't sold.

The thing I remember most about the consultation was the owner's adamant resistance to every suggestion I made. In particular, I told her painting the glossy, deep eggplant blue walls in the dining room would positively alter the direction of the entire space. I remember her firm reply, "As long as I am living in this house, that dining room will always be purple!" Not to sound lippy here, but my thought was, "Well, I hope you really do love it, because you're going to be looking at those same purple walls for a very long time." (I said, I only thought it. I didn't actually say it out loud.) The point being, she didn't want to live there anymore, she wanted to live somewhere else. So, what difference would it have made to her if she just bit the bullet and painted the darn walls? That simple modification alone would have made an enormous impact. But it was extremely clear to me, she would have none of it. I could not convince her to paint. I could not convince her to get rid of the heavy drapes. I could not convince her to pull up a few area rugs. Nothing I said mattered. Basically, I had been paid to give her advice she did not want to hear and chose not to follow.

Several months later I ran into the realtor at the grocery store, and I just had to ask about that house. He said the owner never did make any of the changes and was so frustrated that she finally took it off the market. There she was, still living in that same home and enjoying those glossy purple walls, no doubt. I found it completely baffling. Knowing full well what had already transpired, I decided to give her a call. Upset over the entire experience, she confessed she had absolutely lost her will to move! Honestly, I felt bad for her and asked if she would like to give it another try at no additional cost. I knew staging her home wouldn't take me long. But more so, out of my own selfish pride, I knew I could help if she just gave me the chance! This time, she was more than open to the offer.

One sunny afternoon not too long after, the realtor and I met the owner at her front door. In less than an hour and a half, the three of us had given the house a dramatic makeover. All those changes she was so opposed to,

were welcomed willingly and with a smile. And the icing on the cake, over the weekend the dining room had been painted a crisp, clean shade of creamy linen white. It looked fabulous! I advised the realtor to re-list for $5,000 higher than the first time around. Enough for the owner to recover my previous fee, the paint job, and a little something extra to pad the deal.

Two days later she had an offer. Three days later, she had another. And five days later she accepted an offer for $1,500 under list, which was still $3,500 over the original asking price! Now, how's that for marketing ingenuity? The owner had recovered her entire staging investment and still came out money ahead. But more importantly, the house was SOLD! And the owner was thrilled! Eventually, I went on to help her decorate her new home. And in case you are curious, yes. She had her new dining room painted a glossy, eggplant blue as well. Some things never change.

I've said it before and I'll say it again. When you put your home on the market, it immediately becomes a product, and you need to treat it as such. One of the most frequent complaints I hear from realtors is how unwilling their clients are to make any changes. They insist on keeping the walls eggplant blue. They can not bear to live without three sofas in the living room. Moving the big screen T.V. out of the kitchen is just not an option. But if you really want to sell your home and get the best price for it, you are going to have to put your personal feelings aside and sometimes, your own convenience. It's a lesson you really don't want to figure out the hard way, six months down the road. Open your mind and make the changes before you list your house. A small price to pay considering the potential outcome.

BEFORE Like many older homes, the master bedroom of this country farmhouse left little room for rearranging. To add to the problem, its slanted ceiling and plaster board walls made it difficult to move furnishings or hang artwork. As a result, the brightly covered bed spread took on too much power! The center of attention in this room was the bed, and with a cluttered corner and messy dresser, it was hard to see the actual room.

IN SUCH A SMALL MASTER BEDROOM, IT IS IMPORTANT TO MAKE THE SPACE FEEL MUCH MORE OPEN!

AFTER Without actually moving either of the main furniture pieces, a completely different look is achieved. The first step was to clear out the clutter! A carefree dresser top makes a big impact on the buyers first impression of the room. The small book shelf was brought up from the living room to serve as a height variance to the space, as well as break up the green color scheme.

BEFORE From this straightforward view, it is easy to see how small this room actually felt. The bedding alone seemed to take up too much space! A wastebasket and scale seen peeking out from under the dresser added to the unkept feel.

AFTER By using understated adornments and toning down the bedspread, the eye is actually allowed to see the room without interruption. While a vacant room is certainly not the goal, the smaller the room, the less complicated the décor should be. Thoughtful touches including throw pillows and a soft blanket, along with a small arrangement of colorful chrysanthemums, keeps the space feeling homey. In less than 20 minutes, this awkward bedroom was easily transformed!

AFTER Rather than letting the bed stand out on its own, the cover was flipped over to reveal its basic underside. Inexpensive pillow cases in a pale shade of tan stand in for fancy pillow shams. Throw pillows dress up the bed without grabbing too much attention. The black steamer trunk was pulled out of the opposite corner to add contrast to the setting. A throw blanket was tossed over the top of the trunk to soften the look.

BY PULLING THE SHOWER CURTAIN CLOSED, THIS DIMINUTIVE BATHROOM FELT EVEN MORE CONFINED.

BEFORE A small, dated bathroom was not the owner's favorite room in the house! A large bath mat took over most of the floor. To play down the tub, the shower curtain was pulled shut to hide it from view. A messy vanity always plants negative thoughts in a buyer's mind.

"Keep shower curtains or sliding shower doors 1/2 to 3/4 open to allow for an unobstructed view."

AFTER Removing the bath mat makes the room feel more spacious. A new shower curtain was purchased to add color and reflect the accent tile squares in the floor. Rather than concealing the tub, the curtain is pulled open by half to allow buyers a closer look. An arrangement of silk greenery in a ceramic container adds a little life to the corner.

A WELL SIZED FAMILY ROOM
TOOK VERY LITTLE EFFORT TO
SHOW ITS TRUE POTENTIAL.

AFTER Furnishings were rearranged, creating a more inviting, user-friendly appeal. By pulling the lounger back a few feet, it was easy to create a more open flow. With the sofa out of the way, the table and chairs feel less clunky and obtrusive, and more at ease within the room.

BEFORE A new addition on this home made a nice family room feature and added much in extra living space. But the heavy oak table, used for games and casual dining, bumped up directly to the couch. With the back of the sofa greeting all who enter, this room felt less family friendly than its initial intent. While navy blue walls may not appeal to everyone, it is actually the many hunting trophies adorning the space that were sure to prove a turn off to most.

BEFORE The combination of fireplace and television set felt detached from the rest of the space. Like many informal living areas, this room was purposely built for relaxing and family time. But the layout of the furniture left an awkward space in the middle of the room and seemed to lead directly to the towering corner display.

AFTER Placing the sofa 12 inches from the wall keeps it from blocking the entry view. By arranging the club chair and ottoman a little closer to the center of the room and at an angle, the space that once felt like a path to the corner has been interrupted. This change further allows the fireplace to become part of the setting rather than its own individual entity. To further attract the eye to the fireplace and take a little focus off the television, a bright potted fern was placed at the base of the hearth. Removing additional clutter makes this room feel cleaner, crisper, and more approachable.

LUXURY
LAKE HOME

BUILT ONLY YARDS FROM THE shoreline on a very private lake, this home has much to offer any potential buyer. A large open floor plan, a downstairs recreation room featuring both billiards and a granite-topped bar, and direct water access combine beautifully to make this the ultimate home for leisure! However, too many effects and rooms that felt awkwardly out of balance did little to enhance the homes finer qualities. To play to these features, furnishings were rearranged and reinvented to define distinguished areas. Thoughtfully placed artwork and a few bold strokes of color complete the look. With a little ingenuity, this Luxury Lake Home was completely transformed into the premiere show-off property it was meant to be!

Luxury Lake Home   147

A GRAND FOYER SHOULD BE ALLOWED TO SPEAK FOR ITSELF! USING MINIMAL ADORNMENTS ALLOWS THE DETAIL OF THE SPACE TO BE BROUGHT INTO FOCUS.

BEFORE The view into the main entry shows how a cluttered hallway table and coat rack teamed up to block the staircase and distracted from the wood floors and features of this space.

AFTER By removing the offending elements and pulling up the throw rugs, the focus goes back to the woodwork. Bold foyers demand bold accessories! To make that point, the silk floral arrangement on the landing was easily created using a wicker container found empty in the living room and bright orange and green stems. The colorful display adds enough drama to the entry without distracting. A confident announcement letting visitors know they have arrived!

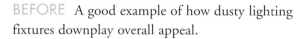 A good example of how dusty lighting fixtures downplay overall appeal.

AFTER By cleaning the lighting in this entry, additional sparkle makes the foyer seem even more grand!

"LIGHTEN UP!"

One thing I frequently notice in homes, whether staging them for market or just visiting friends . . . don't you feel sorry for my friends . . . is that people do not keep their light sources clean! OY!! For taking on such an important role in everyday life, lighting fixtures have got to be the single most ignored element when it comes to cleaning. If a bulb burns out, it is pretty obvious that the room is suddenly darker. But the slow build up of dust and dirt seem so subtle, most never realize its effect. On that same note, there is nothing more disgusting than looking up at a ceiling light only to see the many little decaying carcasses of unsuspecting bugs! GROSS! While not the most convenient task to take on, the payback of sparkling lighting will easily come back to you ten fold. You'll be amazed at the difference! Usually, a sturdy ladder, a spritz of glass cleaner, and a couple of paper towels are all you need to accomplish your goal. Of course, make sure the light is off before you attempt. And call in a professional service if the light is in an out-of-the-way or extremely high location. But for the most part, homeowners can do this on their own with modest effort.

My advice to those of you who have fallen for the old "leave every light in the house on for showings" rule is don't you believe it! Leaving every light on gives a home all the cozy, charming appeal of an asylum, and that is not what you want. No one ever looks their most flattering in stark, bright light. Why do you think candlelight dinners are so popular? The same rule applies when it comes to your house. When lighting for showings, a nice balance of natural lighting, overheads, and table or floor lamps for drama is really the best way to enhance your setting. You are trying to set a mood, here. So, pretend you're getting ready for a hot date, a hot date to sell your house! When it comes to staging your home for market, pay attention to lighting. It will play to your advantage, every time!

AFTER A new furniture layout helps soften the line between the window and the rest of the room. Bringing the furniture away from the carpet's edge and rearranging to welcome buyers rather than hinder them helps to tone down the harsh discrepancies. By drawing the furnishings in, carpeting is now visible behind the sofa and adds to the feeling of spaciousness. The sectional was separated, making the pieces easier to work into the room. The smaller sections were rearranged to invent a more user-friendly design. Rather than losing much needed light, an end table and lamp found a new home between the sofa sections.

BEFORE The view from the foyer into the living room shows how the massive window took over the space. From this angle, the large picturesque window felt like it was a separate entity. A furniture arrangement bordered the perimeter and the back of the sectional sofa obstructed access, which added to a room that seemed uncomfortably heavy on one side and curiously empty in the middle. A straggly Ficus tree felt desperately out of place and drew negative attention.

AFTER With the new arrangement, the illusion of space is created. The sofa was intentionally pulled 18 inches from the window to invite a closer look at the lake. A small seating arrangement was fashioned next to the window to balance out the weight in the room. In the foreground, lamps were flip-flopped with lighting from the bedroom. The heftier bases help stabilize this rooms strong features. By replacing the horizontal artwork over the mantle, the new artwork, purposely chosen for its contrast and vertical appeal, draws the eye in rather than away from the fireplace. Simply placing the mantle grouping closer together creates enough gap to distinguish the fireplace from the rest of the built-ins. To play this up further, adornments on the upper ledge and bookshelves were reduced to keep the eye focused in the center and make the room feel more open. Brightly colored throw pillows and silk flowers borrowed from the entryway arrangement create an easy consistency and break up the green walls.

BEFORE Looking into the living room from the kitchen showed the fireplace with its beautiful marble surround and the built-in entertainment center and shelving. But cluttered bookshelves and a mantle display that falls flat made it hard for the buyer to really see the room itself. The eye was drawn too far around without having any precise line of concentration. It was easy to see how this furniture arrangement lined the perimeter, leaving the center of the room empty and drawing the view away from the features.

AFTER   A closer look at the new seating design shows how easy it was to create. The artwork, reflecting a lakeside scene, brings both color and light to the wall. Rather than investing in new artwork, the piece was borrowed from the owner's office. An antique chair was brought up from basement storage. And a nightstand, one of two, was borrowed from the master bedroom to help free up bedroom space and take on a new role. Had the space on this wall been left vacant, the room would feel lopsided. The heavy oak nightstand helps anchor the weight of the room, and the accessories help add life, making the entire space feel usable.

AFTER   Through thoughtful design, a
visually interesting transition from the
living room to the kitchen is created!

"Using bright shots of color sparingly helps draw the eye into the room without overpowering."

AFTER By replacing the counter chairs with additional stools from the downstairs bar area, the center island is now in the spotlight. Removing the grapevine above the cupboards and replacing it with several smaller displays adds enough interest to grab the buyers' attention and allow them to see the entire space. The decorative bottles that had previously lined the top of the cupboards were brought down and displayed on the countertops for color. Clustering the groupings and purposely creating gaps with visible wall space in between makes the counter space feel expansive.

BEFORE From the living room to the kitchen, the center island is blocked by bulky counter chairs. The silk grapevine and decorative bottles above the cupboards forced the eye to draw a direct line across the top of the cabinetry.

Countertops filled with everyday kitchen staples looked messy, as does the refrigerator door with its many clippings. A doggie dish and scatter rug added to the clutter.

LACKING THE IMPACT OF COLOR OR CONTRAST, THIS DINING ROOM COULD NOT GRAB OR HOLD THE ATTENTION IT DESERVED.

AFTER Without the tablecloth, the exposed glass top reflects light around the room and adds visual interest to the setting. The chairs were simply placed on opposing angles of the table to make the dining set appear larger and fill the space. By packing away three quarters of the contents in the china cupboard, the appearance of storage space is further maximized.

To balance the space, an oak chest from the master bedroom was brought in to anchor the lopsided room. Gloomy plants were replaced by a silk Ficus tree found for under $20 at a discount variety store. The tree was removed from its original plastic pot and steadied in an ornate basket that once served as a waste container in the owner's office.

BEFORE A formal dining room boasting tray ceilings and a built-in china cupboard felt drab and uninviting. The patio dining set seemed informal and too small for the room. A crocheted tablecloth and chair cushions allowed no room for contrast. Overgrown plants only added to the lackluster mood.

AFTER Matching candelabras, a gift to the owner found boxed in a cabinet, adds a touch of elegance. To create an instant centerpiece, one candelabra was teamed with a pillar candle in the same creamy white. For variety, the individual candle was placed on a glass cake pedestal and surrounded by imitation grape clusters.

AFTER To brighten the space, a five yard fabric remnant was purchased in the same vivid colors as the foyer's floral arrangement and living room throw pillows. The fabric was cut four inches wider than the bench cover measurements. It was then folded under, envelope style, and lightly secured with scotch tape to the underside of the lid at the corners. Once the top was closed, the fabric remained in place. This is a simple, temporary trick to add a bright shot of color to a lifeless room. Leftover scraps of the fabric were folded napkin style and tucked into arranged wine goblets in the built-in glass cupboard for an extra boost.

THE KEY TO KEEPING A BUYER'S
INTEREST IS TO THOUGHTFULLY
PLAY UP EXPECTATIONS.

BEFORE A peek down this narrow hallway
leading to the bath and master bedroom felt empty
and dull. A corner knick-knack shelf seemed out of
place. The blank wall felt cold.

AFTER By adding a visual display of
interest down this hallway without over
accessorizing, the eye is drawn subtly in.
This pair of prints from a set of four
purchased at a garage sale brightens the
journey. An antique chair adds mass
without overpowering.

LIKE MANY NEWER STRUCTURES, THE BUILDER OF THIS HOME DID NOT SKIMP ON SIZE OR LUXURY FEATURES IN THIS MASTER BATH.

BEFORE An excessive, spacious bath with its whirlpool tub, double vanity, and custom tiling was easy to enhance!

"There is nothing more appealing than a bathroom that sparkles from top, to tub, to tile!"

AFTER To break the lines between the window frame and vanity mirror, an oversized mirror leaning on the tub surround was stored. Instead, a small print in a bright gold frame allows a distinct flash of wall space to show itself. Vanity clutter was packed away for a nice clean look. A simple vase of yellow blossoms displayed on the counter further fractures the connection between the window and vanity mirror with its non-conforming shape and surge of color.

REDUCING FURNISHINGS AND ACCESSORIES MAKES THIS BEDROOM FEEL BOTH SPACIOUS AND COMFORTABLE.

BEFORE   From the hallway, the view to the master bedroom felt heavy. With a bulky bed frame, symmetrical nightstands, and a mirror too bold for this space, the room was weighed down by its furnishings.

AFTER   To give the room a fresh appeal, a nightstand was moved to the living room. In its place, a plant stand and silk orchid give the corner life. The large mirror was replaced by a more lighthearted arrangement. And by bringing in a few darker taupe throw pillows, the soft bedding is anchored within the space.

AFTER While there was no other location for the dresser, the top was accessorized with a simple display. The framed photo is actually a magazine clipping of flowers. To fill the space left by the video case, which found refuge in a downstairs closet, a small desk chair and vintage family photo were brought in from other rooms. These two enhancements add to a feeling of comfort and ease without getting too personal. While large displays of family photos are never a good idea when it comes to staging your home, one or two nicely framed mementos are certainly acceptable. You should always stay clear of displaying wedding or graduation photos though, as they typically invite a potential buyer to wander off their objective. Any photos used for accessorizing should be kept simple and low-key.

BEFORE From the opposite wall, the line-up of fireplace, cabinet, and dresser were too similar to prove visually interesting. The dresser top and video case distracted with their clutter.

WHEN STAGING A HOME FOR MARKET, EVERY ROOM SHOULD BE CONSIDERED AN OPPORTUNITY TO IMPRESS.

BEFORE Even a laundry room can benefit from a light touch!

AFTER In order to downplay the utilitarian feel of the room, the laundry basket was ordered out. A potted plant and colorful jar of candies help turn this room into a cheerful stop.

"To keep your house spotless for showings, throw wet towels from morning showers in the dryer before you head out. Not only will you keep your bathrooms looking sharp, you will have nice, dry towels at the end of the day!"

THIS GREAT FEATURE ROOM WAS ACHING TO SHOW OFF ITS POTENTIAL!

AFTER To play up this space, the oversized club chair and ottoman went into storage along with the many side tables. Pulling the sofa closer into the room and bringing in a gliding rocker from a spare bedroom helps define the area. A touch of green and boxed board games on the coffee table keep the mood light. By getting rid of the tattered throw pillows and blankets, and clearing off the photos on the sofa table, the room has a crisper, cleaner appeal. The picture over the table was exchanged for two vacation photos of French landmarks which were enlarged 150 percent at a copy center and displayed in store-bought frames. The white matting adds a nice, sharp contrast to the wall space. By resurfacing the pool table, the owner not only set the mood for the room, but also increased the chance of selling the piece with the house!

BEFORE The recreation room in this house had a hard time showing off its potential for fun! With worn furnishings and an unfinished pool table, the space looked frumpy.

THE EFFECTS IN THIS BEAUTIFUL
BUILT-IN BAR AREA WERE
STREAMLINED TO BRING IT
INTO FOCUS.

AFTER Boxing up the clutter gives potential buyers a better idea of how functional this space can be. Stool cushions were removed and a colorful movie poster replaced the framed memorabilia on the wall. Through softer accessorizing, countertops have taken back their stand.

BEFORE While the built-in bar with granite-topped counter were certainly great features on their own, it was hard to see the full impact of this entertaining element.

"Always conceal bottles of liquor when showing your home for market. Whether in a bar area or on the kitchen countertop, the idea of liquor in a home can produce a negative connotation for some."

NEW ENGLAND
CAPE COD

WITH NEWLY ADDED FRENCH DOORS leading to a large cedar deck for entertaining and a beautiful picture window overlooking backyard landscaping, part of the charm of this small, New England Cape Cod is the livability of the outdoor space. But the exterior outshined the interior by far. A frumpy furniture arrangement gave rooms an even more cramped feel and downplayed the home's positive features. Busy wallpaper on the dining room and kitchen walls, still intact from a previous owner, added to the diminutive feel. With only two small bedrooms to its credit and many out-of-date essentials, a gloomy shadow was cast over this home's potential. By rearranging furnishings and playing down accessories, rooms were given an open airy floor plan. Minor improvements were made to bring this home up-to-date. To renew the interior and welcome natural lighting in, walls were painted in warmhearted hues of creamy khaki, lively peach, and cheery linen white. With a fresh new backdrop, a relaxing unity between the home's interior and outdoor area was created.

THE FRONT DOOR OF
THIS SMALL CAPE COD
LEADS DIRECTLY INTO THE
DINING ROOM.

AFTER Walls were toned down with a creamy shade of khaki paint, giving the dining room an open airy feel. While moving the buffet was not an option in this case, boxing up a good portion of the collection it displayed makes all the difference. To further enhance this effect, a portion of shelving and woodwork is left exposed. The dining room table was moved out of the direct eye view and rearranged closer to the window area to free up space. To add a splash of color, plates from the owner's collection are used as a wall accessory in place of artwork.

BEFORE In such a small space, the navy blue wallpaper accented with pink roses gave the room an almost cave-like feel. A peek into the kitchen points out the double offense committed by teaming the busy wall covering with an equally chaotic pattern in plain sight of the adjoining room. Against the deep blue shade, the buffet grabbed negative attention by housing a display of too many china plates and accessories. With no room to walk around, let alone for chairs, the table seemed out of place.

"COVER GIRL"

IT TOOK ME MONTHS TO DECIDE WHETHER TO INCLUDE THIS TIP OR NOT, BUT AFTER MUCH PONDERING, I DETERMINED IT WAS NOTEWORTHY. Before I divulge, I just want to say that I already know in the world of professional painting, wall covering, and interior design, what I am about to pass along is going to generate a lot of controversy. So let me first state that I am fully aware, by all professional standards, it is wrong! I know in the decorating world it is a sin that ranks right up there with "coveting thy neighbor." But please, all of you who will be cringing as I relay this tip, do not call, write, e-mail, or berate me about it. Though it may not be the proper thing to do, I still believe it's a good solution in many cases and the lesser of two evils in others. So here I go. *I personally do not believe it is a catastrophic offense to paint over wallpaper.* There. I said it. I have run across many, many homes on the market that have dated wall covering so hideous, it makes me physically want to lay down and cry. And if it brings a tear to my eye, I can not imagine how offensive it must be to the potential buyer. While the best solution is always to remove the offender with a wallpaper steamer or chemical product, it is not always feasible. Though if you are planning to take that route, I highly recommend you contact a professional if you are all thumbs when it comes to home improvement projects. Most certainly, if you have the time, talent, and patience, it is something you could tackle on your own. The project is messy as all get out, but it can be done. However, if removing the wallpaper is simply out of your realm, I want to pass along some tips that have always worked for me. First and foremost, before you proceed, make sure this shortcut is your best solution. That is to say, if you are living in a million dollar neighborhood, painting over wall covering in the master bedroom may not be looked upon too favorably. Consider your market, as well as the room you will be painting. Secondary rooms are the best candidates, though I don't think it is an issue for any room if the room is smaller. But if you are determined to paint over the wallpaper, the following suggestions will help ensure the best results.

1) **DO A TEST SPOT.** Removing the wallpaper might be a whole lot easier than you think, and you should know beforehand how secure it actually is. If there are loose seams, give a light tug to determine the strength of the bond. Or, I suggest saturating an area by using a spray bottle filled with distilled water. In an out of the way corner, try spritzing the wallpaper completely and letting it soak about 5 to 10 minutes. If it pulls up easily, your papered walls are not a good candidate for painting, as the paint will have the same effect, or worse. If it loosens with a little water, it should not prove too tough to remove and you will be better off stripping the paper from the walls.

2) **CLEAN THE WALLS THOROUGHLY.** Just like you should any time you paint, make sure the walls are grease and dust free. There are products on the market especially for cleaning before you paint, or you could try a mixture of vinegar and water. Do not use strong soapy solutions which could leave a film behind, making it even more difficult for the paint to adhere

3) **SECURE LOOSE SEAMS WITH AN ACTUAL WALLPAPER ADHESIVE.** Do not use school glue, craft glue, super bonding glue, or any other type of glue. It may not hold once you paint over it. Or worse yet, as in the case of a super glue adhesive, it will create an even greater issue for the next owner if they ever want to remove the wallpaper.

4) **USE A GOOD PRIMER AS A BASE.** Wallpaper, especially anything vinyl or vinyl coated, does not accept paint too easily. A good primer will hide the pattern of the paper beneath while regular paint may not, forcing you to apply coat after coat.

5) **USE A TEXTURED ROLLER.** Textured rollers give a light grain to the paint as it rolls onto the walls and can help conceal wallpaper seams.

6) **DO NOT OVER PAINT!** Too much paint on the walls may act as a chemical peeler, creating an enormous mess that will cost more time and money to mend than removing the paper would have cost to begin with. Make sure you do not overly drench the walls.

7) **ALLOW SUFFICIENT DRYING TIME BETWEEN COATS.** This rule goes hand in hand with over painting. Remember, these are not typical walls you are dealing with. Once the first coat is applied, it is likely that some of the paint will soak through to the wallpaper adhesive. This coat of paint must dry thoroughly before another coat is applied. If not dry, additional wet paint and pressure from the roller will likely pull the paper off the wall. I strongly recommend waiting at least 8 hours between coats; waiting 24 hours is even better.

8) If any of these tips give you the jitters or you think this may be more than you can handle by yourself, call in a professional to remove the paper for you. Remember, stripping wallpaper before you paint is always the best solution.

By removing the window treatments, light is welcomed in and the detailing of the bay is visible. Moving the small table 12 inches from the window area, along with two of the chairs, gives this room a cozy café charm. To ensure potential buyers wouldn't hit their heads as they came through, the lighting fixture was raised eight inches to allow clearance. An Irish porcelain vase and silk flowers, while too much for the living room coffee table, are the perfect touch in the dining room. Though not ideal, the odd arrangement of the front entry leading into the dining room is significantly enhanced by the new layout. This space now feels manageable.

BEFORE This view from another side of the room exemplifies how frilly, sheer window treatments defused light and hid the wonderful detailing of the bay windows. Chairs lined around the perimeter of the room, rather than at the table, gave potential buyers the instant message, "There is not enough space to actually dine in here!"

THIS KITCHEN SPACE FEELS EQUALLY SMALL AND CRAMPED, GIVING POTENTIAL BUYERS A NOTICEABLE NEGATIVE SIGNAL.

AFTER To energize the space, busy walls were painted in pale linen. Clutter was cleared from countertops and replaced by minimal accessories and greenery. Likewise, excess above the cupboards was boxed, and the space was adorned with only a basket and spray of silk flowers. Glasses hanging over the sink were washed to remove dust and add sparkle. Once the curtain was removed, more light was allowed in, warming up the room significantly. The window frame and trim were painted white to match the woodwork throughout the rest of the house. As a result, the kitchen feels bigger and more inviting.

BEFORE With strong patterned wallpaper and clutter on the counters and above the cupboards, this small kitchen felt incredibly claustrophobic. Lace curtains blocked light. Hand towels displayed on every available latch, throw rugs, a refrigerator door displaying pictures and coupons, and a dog dish in the corner lent to the dated feel.

This face-lift was taken one step further by shining the cupboards with an orange oil polish designed to enhance the natural wood grain. Once cleaned with the oil soap and allowed to thoroughly dry, the orange oil was then smoothed on with a clean rag. After permitting a few minutes for the oil to soak in, excess was wiped off using a soft dry cloth. With the process complete, it was time to replace the hardware. Instead of using the same dated ceramic knobs, brushed nickel fixtures were applied. Purchasing two packs in bulk at just under $19 for each 18 piece set, the quality of the new hardware was an absolute steal for the price! With the minimal amount of time and cash it took to boost the appeal of this cabinetry, the effort was well worth it. The homeowner was absolutely stunned by the results! The cupboards appear almost brand new. This minor rejuvenation makes the kitchen appear at least ten years younger!

AFTER In addition to painting the kitchen walls, the cupboards benefited from a face-lift as well. Before starting on this project, ceramic knobs were removed. The cabinetry was then cleaned with an oil based soap made especially for wood, removing the grimy build up that had dulled the finish over time.

AFTER To help augment the size of this tiny room, the cheery linen paint color used in the kitchen was repeated in the breakfast area for consistency. The mug rack and collection were removed. The jumble on the corner cabinet was boxed in favor of two more distinct pieces from the owner's crockery collection. The chaos has been transformed into a cheerful spot to enjoy a morning cup of coffee.

BEFORE As you can see, the chaotic effect of the wallpaper continued into the breakfast area. To add to the negative impression, a messy corner built-in and coffee mug collection made the entire space feel unkept.

A VIEW FROM THE LIVING ROOM
INTO THE BREAKFAST AREA
ALLOWS A FULL VIEW OF THE
NEW FRENCH DOORS LEADING
TO THE OUTSIDE DECK.

BEFORE With busy walls and fussy accessories,
it was difficult to appreciate the value of this space.
While it is a wonderful selling point, it took on less
importance due to the colorful wallpaper. A small
cottage table, mimicking the dining room set, held
too much display for its size. Decorative lighting
added to the mix making the space felt muddled.

*"Giving a buyer 'too much to look at'
is overwhelming. Simplify your décor
to keep the focus on the features!"*

AFTER Painting this area a solid color put the attention back on the double doors. Table top adornments were simplified. An area rug, brought in from the living room, serves to break the color between the table set and flooring, and adds a soft texture. The wall clock, previously on display in the living room, connects the short hallway between the breakfast area and kitchen, leading the eye on. Cane chairs were replaced with extras from the dining room set. No longer competing for attention with the wallpaper, the decorative lighting fixture stands out nicely against the new backdrop.

AFTER Angling the loveseat away from the set of windows invites a look at the view. The area rug found a new home in the breakfast room. The heavy cedar chest was placed in storage. In its place, an oak coffee table with lighter proportions, borrowed from a friend's family room, lifts the weight of the furnishings.

BEFORE The expansive trio of windows overlook a well-groomed back yard and gardens, but the walkway to the view is blocked by a massive loveseat. The flat furniture grouping and bulky trunk being used as a coffee table added no visual interest to the space. Placing an area rug over carpeting is a very big no-no! Not only did it break up the flow of the room, it also can make a potential buyer wonder what might be hiding beneath! Built-in shelving displaying too many knick-knacks made the room feel overstuffed and tight for space.

AFTER To give the room some dimension, the sofa was centered on the wall and pulled eight inches into the room. The end table, previously used in the master bedroom, is the perfect spot for the vintage lamp the owner had been storing. By editing the built-in shelving and accessorizing with a few visually weightier pieces, the illusion of space is added. To let in even more light to this dark room, busy valances were removed. Lush green plants add a homey touch.

AFTER To make this room feel more spacious, smaller furnishings found their way to storage. Walls were painted a cheery peach to give a little punch to the walls. The bed was placed at an angle to create walking space into and around the room. The dresser was moved to the opposite side of the wall to allow space for the bed while remaining functional. To tidy up the bedding, the rumpled duvet was removed to show the comforter it protected. Soft colored shams were taken from an old bed set to lighten up the mood. A small, softly patterned quilt found in the owner's linen closet, along with a bright cranberry throw pillow, pull the setting together. The hanging candle, a favorite accessory of the owner, gives a touch of whimsy to the space. By removing the curtains and hanging a new mirror over the dresser, natural lighting is enhanced.

BEFORE An oversized bed crowded a good portion of the room. To further accentuate the tight squeeze, a nightstand, plant stand, and dark framed mirror made this space feel even smaller. With only two small windows, one facing north and the other only steps from the house next door, very little natural light was allowed in. A stenciled border design against the graying walls gave this space a dated feel. Frumpy bedding looked messy, and a sickly plant only added to the dowdy feel.

THIS BATHROOM WAS UPDATED WITH A FRESH COAT OF PAINT AND A FEW MINOR IMPROVEMENTS.

BEFORE A compact bathroom felt even smaller by the outdated stenciling and paint, dark green accessories, and a single window that almost felt as if it had been boarded shut. Wooden towel bars paired up with the vintage cabinet, a cracked mirror over the vanity, and an unflattering, dated lighting fixture made this room look its actual age.

AFTER This close-up shot of the vanity gives you an idea of how minor improvements, including new overhead lighting and a mirror, help to renovate the appeal of the room. As reflected in the glass, a new shower curtain hung with clear rings complete the look.

AFTER Walls were painted with the same linen white from the kitchen and breakfast nook to cheer up the tiny space. The deep green rugs and towels were retired to the linen closet. Flooring was left bare and softer colored towels were hung over a new, brushed nickel towel bar. By losing the valance and opening up the shutters, the space feels much larger. A bright pink arrangement of silk wild flowers is the only splash of color needed.

80's CONTEMPORARY

HOME BUILT IN THE MID-80'S, this structure had very strong design lines, including a living room and master bedroom with soaring ceilings and some very sharp angles. But the furnishings were throwing off mixed signals. While wall coverings, an area rug, and some of the main pieces were screaming contemporary, many accessories were decidedly not. The overall room-to-room flow felt choppy and uneven. To give this home a more defined look and balance, adornments were minimized and stronger enhancements were thoughtfully placed. This attitude was further developed by crafting a cleaner, more open furniture arrangement, complimentary to the original intent of this 80's Contemporary.

AFTER To help take the focus off the wall covering and give the foyer some weight, the hallway table in the entry was flip-flopped with an end table from the living room. The bright red vase and tulips draw the eye to help take concentration off the walls. By removing the slipcovers from the chairs, the clean white fabric and wood combination of the dining set are a sleek attention grabber and prompt anticipation. A shiny green floor plant found a new pot and was brought in from the living room to add a little life to the space.

BEFORE The pattern on the wallpaper was too strong for the entryway accessories and impeded the potential buyer from looking beyond. Red velvet slipcovers over the dining chairs made an unproductive statement and hindered the appeal of the room ahead. The overall lack of pizzazz set an archaic mood.

THIS VIEW GIVES A BETTER UNDERSTANDING OF THE LAYOUT AND IMPACT THIS ROOM HAS ON A BUYER'S FIRST IMPRESSION.

BEFORE From the dining room looking back toward the foyer, the setting felt uninviting and flat. The chairs were too leaden for the room and brought down the mood. A runner and potpourri of small serving dishes did nothing to enhance the built-in glass cupboard feature. From the prospective of the dining room, the wallpaper in the foyer seemed dated.

AFTER Once the velvet covers were removed, the entire ambiance of the dining area shifted! The nice contrast of the upholstery helps the woodwork stand out. To further lighten up the space, the table top was polished to show the reflection of the chairs. The built-in buffet was cleared off and adorned with several more prominent accessories including a shiny brass anniversary clock, a colorful framed photo of an aerial view of the house, and a cheery spring basket of silk flowers found in the living room. By using stronger accessories in place of knick-knack items, the glass cupboard is now a focal point. Looking into the foyer, it is easy to see how the heavier hall table and bright shots of color break up the monotony of wall covering.

BEFORE Looking towards the two-way fireplace shared with the living room shows how the impact of this room could effect a potential sale. Without any fervor, this space may be easily overlooked as "ho-hum!"

AFTER Standing in for the tiresome artwork previously displayed above the fireplace, this vibrant oil painting, while not a favorite of the owner, had been tucked away in an unnoticeable corner of the living room. To keep the focus on and enhance the energy of the fireplace, it turned out to be the perfect replacement. To maintain a keen balance between the blue wall covering and the rest of the space, the colorful area rug is left in place. Vibrant ornamental vases, purchased at under $20 for the two, helps add both liveliness and consistency to the scheme of room. The shiny tabletop is again put to good use as it mirrors the reflection of the colorful vases.

"MAKING SOMETHING OUT OF NOTHING"

SO, YOU'RE ON A TIGHT BUDGET AND YOU DON'T EVEN WANT TO THINK ABOUT PURCHASING ANY NEW ACCESSORIES OR ARTWORK BEFORE YOU SELL? In desperate need of a thing or two, here and there, with no time to waste? You can still come up with some great alternatives with a little innovation. When it comes to accessorizing, there are many things you can get by with in staging that you can't always get by with in everyday decorating. Since potential buyers typically go through a house in under 15 minutes, it is highly unlikely they will inspect your handiwork too closely. And I guarantee, these simple tricks do not require a master's degree in arts and crafts to accomplish.

Try covering pillows with lively fabric purchased by the yard in a clearance bin. Cut the fabric 1 1/2 times larger than the form of your pillow. Fold the fabric envelope style around the form and secure with safety pins. While the back of the pillow is hardly anything you want to show off, the front of the pillow will look just fine! This works equally as well on throw pillows or in place of new shams on bed pillows. You can do the same to well worn seat cushions on chairs. Just make sure not to use them for sleeping or sitting while your house is on the market. Too much rough handling may undo your efforts.

Longer yards of lightweight material also make great, billowy window scarves. Make sure you have enough fabric to create a fluffy effect. Completely unfold the piece you have purchased and throw it into the dryer with a damp colorfast bath towel, or preferably white, to decrease the wrinkles. If you are replacing heavy drapes, you can loosely wind the fabric, free style, over the curtain rod, making sure to cover it entirely. If you are trying to dress unadorned windows, tension rods are your best friend and very inexpensive to purchase.

I have also used fabric to cover the top of an old chest, folded scraps napkin style and tucked them into wine glasses for an extra little shot of color in a glass cupboard, and inserted fabrics sections into picture frames when there was just no other alternative. At a quick glance, an animated fabric print can easily be mistaken for a small canvas of artwork.

If it is artwork you are looking for, try using photos of landscapes, architectural detail, or close-ups of nature copied from your own collection, a calendar, gift card, or magazine. Take the original to a copy store and ask them to enhance the size using regular photo paper. Display the finished product in old frames you've painted, or inexpensive frames purchased at a discount store. For extra punch, try having the photo copied black and white, and display it in a vibrantly painted frame. If you need something on a larger scale, display the print in a salvaged window you have cleaned up and freshly painted. For a large display on a wall, over a mantle, or in place of a headboard, you could also try using an old French door prepared the same way, or a vintage garden gate, cleaned up and repainted.

Just like walls, paint has a way of giving a fresh new look to everyday objects. I once spray painted an old canister set and several casserole dishes I found at a garage sale in several deep shades of red, earthy brown, and gold. The house I was staging was in desperate need of color and accessories, but the owners were literally on a "no budget" plan. Once painted, the pieces were displayed in groupings or on their own throughout the home. When the project was complete, the faux pieces mimicked fine pottery! Not only did they bring in some very much needed vibrancy, they also helped create a nice consistency from room to room. Cost of the project was $4 for the canister set, casserole dishes, vases, plus three cans of spray paint. Clay pots and baskets, worn out tables and chairs, old mirror frames, jewelry boxes, and the like make for great accessorizing, as well. You can usually find many of these everyday items around your own home or purchase them for next to nothing at yard sales or secondhand shops. With a couple cans of paint, a dash of imagination, and very little effort, there are many objects that can be reinvented to help you stage your home.

If you really need to add some color to your presentation or have an open wall space that could use an extra touch, keep in mind, this is not interior design. This is home staging. And you can easily fill the void by creating something out of nothing if you give it a little thought.

AFTER To create an open layout, the loveseat was arranged to allow access to the rest of the room. By removing the clutter, the room takes on a sleeker appeal. Propping the piano top open adds a feeling of luxury to the space. The floor plant found a new home in the dining room. The pleated lampshade was replaced with a more contemporary version. A tall, silk bamboo tree fills empty wall space while adding a shot of color without overpowering.

BEFORE While the arrangement was open to one side of the room, it closed off the access to the baby grand piano. With the loveseat blocking the path, the room felt crowded and "out of tune." Too many fussy accessories made the space feel jumbled and added to the inconsistent style.

An end table which was too small for the setting was moved to the foyer. The sofa was pulled six inches from the wall for depth, and the loveseat was rearranged to open up access to the piano area on the opposite end of the room. By breaking up the chair set, one was used to create a small reading area in the far corner. The floor lamp was flip-flopped with a colorful, stained glass model from the master bedroom. A covered accent table and paintings were stored. The coffee table came out from under wrap to sport bolder accessories, complimentary to the modern furnishings.

BEFORE This view showing the layout of the living area accentuates the need for clear definition to this distinguished room. A mix of styles, clutter, and muted artwork downplayed the soaring walls and style of this home. To accommodate the piano area on the far side of the room, a new furniture arrangement was definitely needed.

AFTER Not only does the new arrangement clear the path through the room, but the loveseat visually anchors the setting against the intense wall of windows. By applying bolder strokes with the layout and accessories, the focus is now on the room's design features.

AFTER The strong blue accent wall surrounding the fireplace was softened by bringing over one of the conversational chairs. The subtle shades of blue in the upholstery help to soften the stark wall covering and bring it into the room. To return the focus to the fireplace, a colorful but less obtrusive adornment was used to accentuate the wall.

BEFORE From this side view, the influence of the home's design is even more apparent. The congested feel of the furniture and accessories was too meek for the backdrop. Too many heavy furnishings on one side of the room, in this case the piano and loveseat, made the rest of the space feel disproportionate. A dried wreath over the fireplace looked dated and out of sync with the furnishings and detracted from the fireplace.

TO MAKE THIS KITCHEN FEEL MORE
CONTEMPORARY, ACCESSORIES
ARE USED SPARINGLY.

AFTER Excess was removed from the
shelves and countertops, leaving only a
few choice groupings in place. By
streamlining the rooms effects, the
kitchen takes on a more updated feel.
A blooming pot of white chrysanthemums
and a vase of bright red tulips, the same
shade as those in the foyer, add a nice bit
of cheer to this dark oak room.

BEFORE A very basic kitchen touting forest green
countertops fought against the contemporary style of the
home with its clutter and heavy country scheme.

AFTER By ridding the far wall of adornments harmonizing with the green color scheme and lifting up the table cloth and area rug, the country motto of this room is downplayed. A set of matching pictures in mahogany frames with blue matting are displayed on the same hangers as the previous accessories to avoid creating more holes in the wall. A dog dish and bed were relinquished to an out of the way spot in the basement while the house is being shown. Simple enhancements give this area an open and spacious feel, favorable to the mood of the rest of the house.

BEFORE The wall covering, coordinating plaid table cloth, and sunflower print on the wall lended a country feel to this room.

AFTER This kitchen view shows how using effects sparingly can open up the overall appeal of a space.

AFTER By simply walking through and boxing most of the owner's pictures and knick-knacks, the functionality of the room took front seat. The recliner and rug found refuge in a basement storage room. In place of the bulky lounge chair, seating with a modern flair was brought in from a secondary room.

BEFORE The family room felt overstuffed. Too many family photos lining the wet-bar invite a potential buyer to snoop. A colossal lounge chair facing the cluttered entertainment center was too much for this small space. The area rug hindered the flow of the room. Generally, an area rug over carpeting is not recommended when showing a house since it may offer the perception of concealing possible issues.

Heavy editing allowed the family room freedom without hindering the owner's comfort. The oversized sofa was pulled into the room by nearly three feet. This simple step offered potential buyers a closer look at the view outside by allowing them free access to the windows. It also assisted in drawing the eye to the fireplace by framing the hearth. Silk greens, previously greeting visitors at the top of the staircase, further enhances this focal point. The stained glass floor lamp was moved to the downstairs living room and a sleeker brass floor lamp, found in the master bedroom, was brought into the setting. By ridding the room of excess furnishings, the area rug, and adornments, an unspoiled view of the actual space and room design is achieved.

BEFORE The straightforward view of the fireplace revealed how distracting the furnishings were and how little space there seemed to be.

SOARING WALLS AND SUNNY WINDOWS ARE A GREAT FEATURE IN THIS SPACIOUS MASTER BEDROOM.

AFTER To put the focus back on the room, the wall hanging was replaced by something less overpowering. Bedding was simply straightened up and augmented with a few pillows and a throw in a pale shade of taupe giving the bed a cozy feel. Rather than contrasting, the neutral colors of the new accessories compliment the wall color, and tone down the strong pink hue. A small nightstand, bedside table, and lamp duo were moved out of the room to free up the perimeter around the bed, making the space feel larger. An alternate floor lamp, flip-flopped from the downstairs living room, coordinates with the new scheme. A trio of vacation photos in a sharp, steel frame serve to modify the grouping. The table lamp on the dresser is from the upstairs family room.

BEFORE A bright silk-screened print hanging on the wall solely dominated the viewer's attention, rather than enhancing the soaring ceiling of the master bedroom suite. The strong pink color of the artwork made the pink paint on the walls standout. With mismatched furnishings and a juxtaposition of decorating styles, it was hard to concentrate on the positive.

BEFORE A storage chest in front of the window
and covered by a blanket blocked a close view to the
balcony. The multi-colored window treatments
proved distracting and too harsh for the easy palate
of the room.

AFTER The chest was pushed out of the
way and carried to basement storage
creating an open path to the windows.
By replacing the colorful drapes with
sheer taupe window scarves, the
presentation is softened.

THE DATED WALLPAPER AND
WATER DAMAGE TOOK AWAY
FROM THE APPEAL OF THIS LARGE
MASTER BATHROOM.

BEFORE In comparison to the master bedroom,
the bathroom felt stark and lifeless. Leaky plumbing
left a noticeable blemish on both carpeting and
access panel.

AFTER Plumbing issues were fixed and
the damaged components replaced.
Personal items around the tub were
tucked away in cabinets. To warm up
the space, a chenille bath mat and new
towel set, along with lively green plants,
were added. The picture over the tub
came from the family room. Paler colors
in the print reflect the soft tones of the
master bedroom.

BEFORE Messy countertops are unattractive. The stark green sinks looked dated and drew too much attention.

AFTER Simply clearing the clutter and bringing in a lush, full plant and coordinating hand towels give this room a totally fresh outlook. By using differentiating shades of green, the dual sinks don't feel out of place with the rest of the bath area.

WHERE DO I START?

Where do I Start?

That's always the question, isn't it? Now that you've paged through examples and hopefully have an idea of what you are trying to achieve, all you need is a game plan! It's actually a lot less complicated than you think. Once you have established what elements you should play up and what you should play down, it's merely a matter of digging in and getting it done.

There are typically four areas of any home that affect a potential buyer's decision, and these areas should always receive the majority of your attention. This is not to say you should leave the rest of your home as is. But when I am professionally staging a home for market, these areas are always the spaces I concentrate on first and they are usually the most time-consuming.

Foyer or Entry - All rooms directly visible from the main entrance are a priority. This is the potential buyer's first impression of your home, and it is always number one on my list, no matter what. You need to create a visually appealing atmosphere the moment a prospective buyer steps in the door. Keep in mind, they will be forming an opinion within seconds. And the first thing they notice, positive or negative, is going to set the pace for the rest of the showing. You definitely need to make sure your home grabs them from the start. If not, you're going to be facing a tough uphill battle to win them over. Whether your front door leads into a large marble foyer or steps directly into the living room, any area visible from the main entry has got to be sharp.

Main Living Area - Whether it is a formal living room, family room, or combined space, the main living area is basically the place that people will spend most of their time, entertain guests, etc. Its importance is quite obvious. This space typically takes the most time to finesse. Furniture arrangement and accessory placement is a priority for this area.

Kitchen - People spend a lot of time in the kitchen as well. A clean, good-looking, and efficient space is always quite desirable. The more workspace you can show, and the lighter and brighter you can make it, the more functional and cheery this area will feel. The kitchen is usually an important consideration for most.

Master Bedroom - A master bedroom is oftentimes the only area in the house that the owner can truly stake claim to as their own personal territory, and they take their personal territory pretty seriously. Your goal in the master bedroom is to make it as comfortable, carefree, and relaxing as possible.

Feature rooms such as a family room, loft space, den, study, or sun room are always next on my list. While bathrooms are very important, a good cleaning is usually the main factor. Play them up, but don't go over the top when it comes to accessories. Laundry rooms, pantries, closets, and cupboards should also be maintained. Especially if you have a little overload going on. I typically tell my clients to concentrate on main closets, such as those found in the entryway, master bedroom, bathrooms, or a linen closet. I guarantee, people will want to see what kind of space you have, and many are going to pull open a door to take a look. I usually advise homeowners to eliminate anywhere from half to three-fourths of what is inside for the best presentation, and sometimes, even more. Show off as much space as possible. It is important to stage secondary rooms such as a kid's room or spare bedroom as well and make sure they look clean and spacious. Getting rid of the clutter and excess furniture is usually enough to make an impact, though a new arrangement and a few enhancements may be in order.

Any main room or feature room, such as a living room, dining room, or master bedroom should always be set up to play to the function of its original design. That is to say, if you are currently running your home office out of the formal dining room, it needs to be transformed back into a formal dining room. Potential buyers are going to be walking in with certain expectations. If a formal dining room is part of your home's design, you need to show that to the buyer. That's what you are selling, and that is what they came to see. Otherwise, you will be giving the impression that the house is simply out of space and needed to be modified to be functional. If you have turned an extra bedroom into a home office, that's fine. As long as it's neat and tidy, and as long as you have other bedrooms to endorse.

On that same note, any spare room with no real use should be shown as livable space. The same goes for completely empty rooms. I have seen many homes using those extra rooms as storage. Fine and dandy while you're living there, but it's not exactly going to impress a potential buyer. The more functionality you can show, the better. Transforming the room into usable square-footage is always the better option and very easy to accomplish. Bed frames are cheap, and an air mattress can take the place of the real thing in a pinch. Combined with a chair or a couple of extra furnishings and accessories from other rooms you have already staged and you can easily show-off a useful space. Buyers don't want to have to imagine it; they want to see it. As an absolute last resort, I don't think it's the worst thing in the world to store a little excess in a secondary room by stacking anything leftover very neatly in an out-of-the-way corner. You can probably get by with it if the rest of the house is in top form. People are forgiving of a few boxes if they don't take over the house. But if you simply have too much to store and no place to go with it, renting a storage unit is an extremely good investment.

The key to successfully staging your own home is looking at it objectively with the potential buyer in mind. View your house as they might view it and completely remove yourself of emotional attachment. This is sometimes easier said than done. But remember, your house is now a product, and you need to view it as such. The first step is getting yourself in the right frame of mind! The entire idea is to show your home off and sell it quickly for the highest profit. The less you personally connect, the better off you will be. Although you may be comfortable with your furnishings and effects as they are presently arranged, your current set-up may not be the best way to show off the house itself. Once you realize this and are prepared to do what it

takes to get it in the best condition, the rest is really quite easy.

1) ASSESS YOUR HOME!

Walk through the house just like a prospective buyer would. Take the same route. As you walk through, make a list of features that are your home's positive selling points or focal points. These are elements of the house that make it unique, give it character, or might be considered a bonus to the potential buyer. Selling points must be actual fundamentals of the structure itself, such as a grand foyer, designer windows, a fireplace, built-in shelving, large walk-in closets, beautiful wood flooring, or an open floor plan, to name a few. All of these would be considered selling points, and you want to play them up. Most homes have at least one or two elements that would be considered positive features.

Next, consider what might be looked at negatively. Negatives to consider aren't always an actual part of the structure. In fact, they are often decorating elements or personal effects. When I do an initial walk through of a home, I use what I call my peripheral vision. I take in everything without really focusing on anything in particular. Whatever catches my eye is usually something that needs work. Small cramped space, clutter, worn carpeting, wild wall covering, dated essentials such as lighting fixtures, or a monotonous furniture layout are just a few things that might be considered off-putting. Add them to your list as well and keep all these elements in mind.

Staging your home is much easier once you understand the positive and negative aspects of the actual house. Knowing these also helps to give you a clearer understanding of where to start and what you need to accomplish. While you never actually want to hide anything that might be viewed as off-putting, playing up the positive aspects often deters from the negative aspects in the process.

2) BOX UP CLUTTER!

Boxing up superfluous effects is the next step to preparing your home. Getting rid of the muddle will make the rest of your efforts much more efficient. Typically, I have clients make one run through the entire house, boxing up unnecessary adornments or anything that takes up too much space or looks messy. You will likely notice a major change in the perception of your home by this assignment alone. For further information on clutter removal, please re-visit "Clutter-Bug" in Chapter Two California Ranch.

3) RENEW, REPAIR, OR REPLACE!

Once you've boxed up excess, now is the time to take a good look at the basics. Without all the clutter in your way, it is easier to decide what you need to renew, repair, or replace. Remember, "you get what you pay for." And everyone knows it. If you expect to receive a decent offer for your home, you need to give the buyer a decent product in return. Potential buyers like to feel that your home has been well maintained, and part of this process is making sure it looks the part. A common mistake homeowners often make is assuming a prospective buyer won't notice the scruffy carpeting, will look past the broken light fixture, or will not even realize that stain on the wall is from water damage. Well, I hate to tell you this, but they will notice! And you need to get rid of all that ails before you start inviting people in to take a look.

Oftentimes, a thorough cleanup will be enough to create the right image. Just like the kitchen cupboards in the New England Cape Cod, a light

face-lift is usually pretty easy to accomplish and makes a big impact without spending a lot of money. Repairing any obvious damage is a given. Leaving the issues for all to see is not an option. If something is damaged or worn-out and can be repaired, do not hesitate to have it restored. But if renewing or repairing does not do the trick, it is usually best to replace. I can't tell you how many times I've advised a homeowner to replace desperately stained carpeting or repaint scratched and scuffed walls, only to be told they don't want to pay for something they won't be using. Well, that kind of thinking could not be more wrong. As any good investment broker will attest, you have to spend money to make money. And the same is certainly true of your house.

Just like any investment, you have to exercise common sense and good judgment to execute a winning venture. For instance and as an extreme example, if you have been planning to knock out a wall to expand your kitchen, now is not the time. The money spent and time involved would not be recovered if you're planning on selling your house in a month. However, if your kitchen countertop has been scraped, chiseled, and burned beyond recognition, replacing it would be a smart move.

You have to be thoughtful about where you invest. If a feature is not there now, no one is going to miss it. But if it is an existing blemish, something must be done. While I am by no means suggesting you go crazy and take out a second mortgage just to get rid of the first one, you do have to realize what hindrances might be standing in the way of a decent sale price. Take the time and use your common sense to invest wisely.

Walls - Scuffs and scratches can usually be cleaned up with a light solution and water. A soft-scrub cleanser can remove deeper marks from light painted walls. In any case, you never want to scrub too hard, or you may end up removing the paint. When using a solution or cleanser, be sure to test a discreet area first to ensure you don't permanently discolor the wall. If there is just too much damage to clean up, your best bet is to repaint. Do this before you actually stage the rooms you are painting, since it will require you to basically remove everything during the process.

Doors, Trim, and Woodwork - Like walls, if paint or stain is chipped or scuffed, repainting or restaining should be done first. A freshly painted, glossy front door never hurt anyone's chances to impress a prospective buyer! Make sure all knobs and locks are in working order. If they are not, repair or replace them as well.

Carpeting - Even if your carpeting is in good condition, it should still be professionally cleaned. Stay away from any type of shampooing method, as this will only grind the dirt in deeper and leave a heavy soap residue that is very dulling. A good rinse-and-vac type system is my recommendation. Your carpeting will have a new look and feel, as this method will efficiently clean, pull up, and re-vitalize the fibers, as well as eliminate any odors that might be lurking within. If your carpeting is permanently stained, extremely worn, or dated, it should be replaced. Ditto when it comes to linoleum or other such flooring.

Sinks, Tubs, Toilets, and Shower Stalls - Stained porcelain and tile cleans up nicely using a soft-scrub cleanser with bleach. There are also some great products on the market to help eliminate hard water

spots or corrosion caused by calcium, lime, and rust build up that can be used on porcelain, stainless steel, and some chromes. Garbage disposals should also be tested to ensure they work. Replace anything that can not be cleaned or repaired.

Faucets - Again, hard water spots and corrosion can be cleaned up with a product especially formulated for this purpose. If you have a leaky faucet, a 10-cent washer may do the trick. But if the faucet can not be cleaned or fixed, exchanging for new will be a positive upgrade. Likewise, many basic spray heads or shower heads can easily be replaced.

Appliances - This includes stoves, ranges, overhead fans, refrigerators, dishwashers, built-in microwaves, washers, and dryers. Especially important if the appliance is being sold with the home, it should be super clean, inside and out. I guarantee, someone will inevitably inspect them. For self-cleaning ovens, be sure to remove the oven racks to prevent damage during cleaning. Replace crusty looking drip and broiler pans. Make sure all appliances are in working order. If an appliance is being sold with the house and is not in working condition, replace it. Appliances go on sale all the time. A basic model, in this case, is usually a worthwhile investment.

Lighting Fixtures - This is a big issue with me! Clean them up and replace burned out bulbs. If the fixtures are broken or dated, I can not stress enough what a difference this could make in your presentation. You don't have to buy top-of-the-line for an upgrade. Try the discount home improvement centers for an inexpensive and up-to-date replacement. While you're at it, make sure all the switch plates are in good condition, nothing cracked or broken.

Windows - Windows should always be cleaned. The same goes for screens. While a good vacuuming is often sufficient, for really dirty screens, remove them for a long spray under the garden hose and a little soapy scrub with a soft-bristled brush. If possible, leave them out of the windows altogether for showings. This will provide additional natural lighting. Make sure to mark each screen for easy replacement when it comes time to put them back. Broken glass should be replaced; ripped screens should be repaired. And do not forget about the window casings. They can get extremely dirty and dusty. Usually, a good vacuuming and wiping with a damp rag will suffice. If the paint is full of nicks and scratches, they should be repainted.

4) EDIT AND REARRANGE FURNITURE!

Furniture placement is extremely important when staging your home. The layout of your furnishings will dramatically effect the way potential buyers will identify with the space. This is usually the toughest part of the staging process for many. Beginning with the four areas of your house that will most affect a buyer's decision and working your way down the list is an efficient and deliberate method. Refer to your home assessment list and decide specifically what you need to play-up or what might be seen as a negative.

Editing furnishings is frequently an ongoing process to create the right balance. Obviously, there are going to be pieces that will just have to stay where they are. A cumbersome glass cupboard, a heavy entertainment center, or an over-sized bed and frame might be pieces you would not be able to move or simply have no other place to put. In that case, you just have to work around it. No big deal. It is the manner in which you work the piece into the space that's important.

Keep in mind, your furniture arrangement should always play to the focal point of the room. For instance, if a fireplace is the selling point of your living room and your set-up currently evolves around the television set, you will need to redirect attention to the fireplace. You don't want to draw the eye to the T.V., because you are not selling the T.V. The fireplace is what you want potential buyers to notice, and your furniture arrangement should reflect that.

Start with the obvious. In the living room, for example, a sofa, loveseat, and club chair might be the basic furnishings. Placement of these heftier pieces will determine the rest of the layout. It is a rarity that I ever line furniture directly along a wall, unless it is already in place and can not be moved. This monotonous and visually boring arrangement actually makes the room appear smaller rather than larger. By lining furnishings around a room's perimeter, a gawky, open space in the center of the floor that knocks the entire setting out of sync is created. This is not the effect you want. Pulling major furnishings at least eight inches into the room gives the space dimension. While it may seem peculiar to you since that is not how you personally see the space, the new arrangement will add interest and produce a sense of spaciousness that will be very apparent to potential buyers.

Think about what you are doing. Think about what you are trying to show the buyer. Keep your layout open and airy. Add interest through angles, dimension, and height variation. Allow visible wall space behind and between furnishings. Arranging a grouping closer into a room creates a feeling of spaciousness by freeing up the area around it. And framing your furnishings near a focal point draws the potential buyer's attention directly to that detail. You never want the back of major piece to obstruct access

into a room. It blocks the entire flow of the space. And you never want anything preventing a potential buyer from an effortless entry. Make sure rooms appear as sizably generous as you can make them while still maintaining a conceivable level of comfort.

When it comes to the actual furniture, ratty and worn out pieces will either have to be renovated or removed. A shabby looking sofa is incredibly distracting. It also makes a person wonder how well you've been taking care of the rest of the place. If your sofa cushions are worn, try flipping them over. The underside might be in better condition. Even if a zipper on the cushion shows, it will likely not be half as noticeable as tattered and torn upholstery. Most won't even realize it's a zipper, especially if you have achieved the goal of the room and presented a nice layout. A slipcover is also a great quick-fix and a better option than showing unsightly upholstery. Sofa and chair fabrics can also be cleaned. When you have the carpeting done, ask them to do your upholstery as well.

While sectional sofa units are great in some rooms, they are very hard to work with in many, and I seldom find they actually do much to enhance the space. They are simply too big, not to mention attention grabbers. I typically break up the piece to create a more versatile, appealing arrangement with the smaller sections. Two separate sofa segments give you more options to work with than one gigantic lug of a sectional, in tact.

Don't be afraid to flip-flop furnishings between rooms! While you might be accustom to using a piece one way or another, keeping an open mind can resolve many dilemmas. If a room is too heavy on one end, it might need to be anchored with an equally heavy piece on the other side. Consider reinventing furnishings from

other rooms for balance. If your house has no room to room flow, try breaking up a matching furniture set by exchanging elements of it with furniture from other rooms. This is a great way to create continuity in color and style from one space into the next.

Secondary furnishings, such as end tables and side chairs, should be arranged after the main furnishings are in place and used only to compliment the grouping. Just like anything else in the staging process, less is more. Furniture and accent pieces that aren't absolutely necessary to the visual appeal of a room should be removed altogether and stored, or used in another area of your home, when possible.

To ease the strain of moving heavy pieces, invest in a set of Moving Men™, though I am not referring to the kind of moving men you might be thinking of. Moving Men™ are actually a set of gliding discs that have a spongy cushion on one side and a smooth, slippery plastic backing on the other. By placing one disc under each leg or corner of the piece, you can literally glide almost anything across carpeting with very little effort. Personally, I don't have a lot of muscle, but using these discs, I once moved a baby grand piano across sculptured carpeting all by myself! They are incredibly inexpensive, and you can purchase them at almost any home improvement center. You can also get them with a scratch-free backing for hardwood flooring.

When it comes to arranging your furnishings for staging, there are many creative alternatives most people usually never think of. Don't be afraid to experiment. And remember your objective. I have been known to move the same two-ton sofa to half a dozen spots all the way around a room until I got it right. Sometimes I hit it on the first try, sometimes it takes me a few. You just have to keep trying until it falls into place.

5) DRESS FOR SUCCESS!

Unless you were applying for a position as a country western singer, you probably wouldn't show up for an interview with a law-firm in a colorfully embroidered shirt and ten-gallon hat. While you would certainly grab attention, I guarantee it would be negative attention. And you would likely be remembered for your badly chosen attire rather than your actual qualifications. As any career counselor will tell you, dressing appropriately for an interview is an important part of the process. You always want to look the part. This is exactly the theory of home staging. You are preparing your house for one gigantic interview.

You have to remember, when accessorizing your home for show, you are selling the house, not your stuff. You want to make sure the adornments you choose will enhance the space and not distract. If your house is properly staged, enhancements will thoughtfully draw the eye to the real feature without becoming one themselves. Accessories should always be used in moderation and only placed for a purpose. You want them to be subtle, never to be shown off for their own sake. And you don't want to over-do it, too much will simply nullify all the clutter clearing you did to begin with. Just keep repeating to yourself, "Less is more. Less is more. Less is more." Clean sharp lines and a sophisticated simple appeal is the best look when it comes to selling your home.

Heftier, more substantial adornments are a better choice than a lot of muddled knick-knacks. When playing-up a focal point like a fireplace mantle, go for a little drama. A few stronger pieces are eye catching and will direct the line of view to the fireplace. Built-in shelving and cupboards are also better enhanced with fewer adornments to show off the space. To bring interest to a

colorless room, try using a few bright pops of color with throw pillows, artwork, or lush green plants. To downplay strong hues in upholstery, carpeting, or on the walls, go in the completely opposite direction and opt for neutral enhancements.

Artwork should always be placed last. Like any other accessory, use some discretion. You do not have to fill every bit of available wall space. And in fact, you shouldn't! Allowing for a few spots of completely bare wall will give the prospective buyer's eye a place to rest and enhance the illusion of space in a room.

Never hang artwork too high. In other words, if you have to strain your neck to see it, it's too high. As a general rule, artwork should be hung as part of a furniture grouping and at eye level. That means, the center of the artwork is directly at the center of your line of vision. The view that leads a prospective buyer around the room is anchored by furnishings and features, and should move with ease in a gradual sequence. Artwork that has been hung too high creates a second line of vision that will draw the eye to the ceiling. So now, not only have you created a lot of funky, awkward space between the furniture and the artwork, but the potential buyer, who should be checking out the features of the room, is now busy checking out your ceiling for cobwebs.

Obviously, there are always some exceptions to this rule. Oversized works of art or displays over taller mantles are just a couple instances in which this may not apply. Though in either case, the piece should still feel like part of the scheme of the room or thoughtfully displayed on soaring wall space for drama. Another option to hanging art, and a great way to create dimension, is to lean artwork or a decorative mirror against the wall. This can be done on a mantle, buffet, sofa table, or other similar items. Not only will you bring the piece closer into the setting, but you could easily create an element of height to a grouping when needed.

Accessorizing should always be a well thought-out process. Use adornments sparingly and make sure there is always a purpose for their presence. If you are unclear as to how much is enough or how much is too much, lean toward the conservative side.

6) CLEAN!

You should clean your house as though your life depended on it! Though it actually doesn't, a potential offer might. Nothing is more unappealing to a prospective buyer than a dirty house. Even if they are personally living in a pig sty, I guarantee, they are going to nitpick over the way you keep house. It's a given. No one wants to buy someone else's dirt. So if cleaning is not your bag, hire a professional. Though I caution, as with any professional service, there are good ones and bad ones. If you don't know anyone personally, try a little networking with family, friends, and co-workers. It is likely that someone will know someone. If not, there are many cleaning companies out there. I suggest you look for one that specializes in "move outs." They are typically more proficient at the kind of deep cleaning you are looking for. Regardless of whether you do it yourself or hire outside help, create a list of all the things that need to be done and make sure it is followed to the letter. Cleaning your house to sell is a more thorough cleaning than the weekly dusting and vacuuming most people do, and you need to be certain everything is spotless.

Kitchens and bathrooms take priority. You want them to sparkle from top to bottom. And that usually means getting down on your hands and knees to clean-up the nitty-gritty. Along the baseboards, in the corners, cupboard fronts, under a standing sink, and don't forget the toilet! (Under, behind, around, and inside!) Garbage disposal odor's can be easily eliminated with baking soda or by grinding up a few, fresh lemon peels.

I have no doubt, some of those knick-knacks and books you have recently packed away were hiding a lot of dust. While those quick, wipe up cloths that are so popular now have their place as a speedy once-over, they are not good for thorough dusting. Use an actual polish and a clean, soft cloth for woodwork. Everything, and I mean everything, needs to be dusted. Furniture, accessories, picture frames, mirrors, etc., should all be able to pass the white glove test.

When it comes to flooring, an effective cleaning includes getting right up to the walls and deep into the corners. Baseboards and permanent heating or cooling elements should also be given attention.

For cleaning solutions, I recommend you stay away from anything with a strong pine scent. Many people have objections to the smell of pine. It can leave behind a rather medicated, hospital aroma. Opting for a solution with a more fresh breeze or citrus scent is much more appealing to most.

Once your house has experienced a deep cleaning session, it will be much easier to keep it clean while on the market. Just make sure to have that list in hand before getting started so you don't miss a thing!

7) PREPARE TO SHOW!

The more simplistic and efficient your home has been staged, the easier it will be to maintain for showings. For example, a foofy bedspread and multitude of pillows on your bed might make straightening up in the morning a bit of a chore. But an easy white throw with only a pillow or two for color can have you out of the house on time and with very little effort. Fewer accessories and knick-knacks require less dusting. The less clutter you have, the better.

Avoid cooking smelly foods while your house is on the market. Odors from fish, liver, onions, garlic, spicy foods, or anything fried have a tendency to linger in the air. Garbage bins should always be emptied. Throw wet towels and shower mats in the dryer before you leave for work to keep the bathroom looking tidy. And make sure to change the water in a vase full of fresh flowers daily.

While your realtor may be a little more diplomatic, or so afraid of insulting you they fail to mention, I am going to tell you flat out. Kids and pets are both a no-no for showings. I love them both dearly, honest I do. But as cute as they might be, they are a distraction. And you absolutely do not want anything taking a potential buyer's attention from your house. So unless the kids and the pets are part of the deal, they should not be around for showings.

It is especially important that pets are not present during showings. For one thing, it's hard to know how an animal will react to strangers coming into the house when you are not around. I have a 95-pound lap-dog myself. And I can tell you, as loveable as he is around me, my friends, and family, I don't know that he could be trusted alone under those circumstances. Animals get stressed. And if

someone they don't know is waltzing around their territory, they might nip. They might bite. They might scratch. And you might get sued. Another fact you might want to consider is that some people are afraid of animals, and some simply don't like them. Prospective buyers may not be thrilled when they show up at your door in their gray flannel suit, only to have kitty-cat cozying up against their leg the entire showing. They will likely leave with a negative impression and, not to mention, a pant leg full of cat hair. I strongly suggest you remove all pets, and any evidence that they even exist, from the premises. I guarantee, pets in the home can be a deal-breaker.

And finally, unless this is a "For-Sale-By-Owner" property, you shouldn't be there either. Potential buyers will talk more open and candidly to their agent about a property without the owner hanging around. It's uncomfortable. If they have anything they want to ask or comments they would like to make, the viewing is the time they want to make them. It is much better if you vamoose before they arrive. Take the kids and the pets for a drive around the block a few times. Take them to Dairy Queen™ for a treat. Visit Grandma for an hour. Just don't be hanging around your house when it's go time!

8) ASK FOR HELP!

If you don't think you can be objective when it comes time to stage your own home, asking a friend's opinion can be of great benefit in understanding how your house might be seen by an outsider. The friend who will spare your feelings at all costs is usually not the best choice to provide an honest opinion. But the friend who will candidly tell you how your behind looks in those new pair of jeans is a good choice. If you are going to recruit someone to assist,

remember, you did ask! And you should not take offense by their judgment. This is not about you, personally. This is all about selling your house. They have been enlisted to help you out, so be prepared. To avoid conflict or hard feelings, give your friend a few guidelines to follow. Let them know that you value their opinion, what your goal is, and remind them to be gentle, but honest. And remember, they are there to help. If you look at this as a positive thing and keep a sense of humor about you, you will certainly get more out of it than by taking everything they say as a personal attack on your sense of style.

There are also professional home stagers out there who are quite proficient in helping you show your home for market. Most can be hired to do either hands-on staging or to consult and help kick your game plan into high gear! I have a group of Center Stage Home Affiliates in various cities across the U.S. and Canada who have personally trained with me and would be happy to help.

My affiliates are listed in the index of this book, or for current information, you may visit my website at www.centerstagehome.com. If you don't find a Center Stage Home Affiliate in your area, visit www.homestagingexpert.com for a directory of other home staging professionals who have trained with Center Stage Home.

When it comes time to sell your home, first impressions count. And by showing a buyer what they want to see, you are ultimately creating your own opportunity for success. Staging your home before it goes on the market creates the ultimate win-win situation for all involved.

651.220.2746
Visit www.centerstagehome.com
for further information on services,
new affiliates, or opportunities

CALIFORNIA

West LA County
Alberta Moore
(323) 292-5865

COLORADO

Denver
Carolyn Brake
(303) 766-1186

FLORIDA

Tampa
Judy Kincaid
(813) 601-2814

Treasure Coast
Jennifer Mogavero
(772) 201-5043

ILLINOIS

NW Chicago
Jane Douglas
& Kristine Porter
(847) 516-3694

MICHIGAN

NW Detroit
Diane Howard
(734) 358-5883

MINNESOTA

Crookston
Marlys Leiser
(218) 945-6372

SE Mpls/St. Paul
Pam Julin
(612) 715-1284

OHIO

Columbus
Cindi Johnson
(800) 848-7400 ext. 6537

TEXAS

Austin
Marilyn Taylor-Brown
(512) 565-6824

N Dallas
Nancy Peham
(972) 208-4611

Houston
Valerie Splaine
(713) 858-5507

651.220.2746
Visit www.homestagingexpert.com
for Home Staging Workshops, to find other
Home Staging Experts, or to inquire about
Home Staging Training